NOTES FOR ━━ ▪▪▪▪

Peter James Child

Benbow Publications

Published in 2001 by Benbow Publications
PO Box 105, Bedford, MK43 0FA

British Library
Cataloguing in Publication Data.

ISBN : 0-9540910-0-0

Printed by Watkiss Studios Limited, Holme Court,
Biggleswade, Beds. SG18 9ST

First Edition

OTHER TITLES BY THE AUTHOR

VEHICLE PAINTER'S NOTES

VEHICLE FINE FINISHING

VEHICLE FABRICATIONS IN G.R.P.

ACKNOWLEDGEMENTS

I wish to acknowledge all the help and assistance given to me by Sue Gresham, who set out the book, to Stephen Mason for his exacting editorial, to Andrew McArthur and Wendy Tobbit for the cover presentation and to Jim Hutchings for his accurate and amusing cartoons.

Without all these people, Notes for Good Drivers would not have been possible.

AUTHOR'S DRIVING CV

- Passed Driving Test in May 1958
- Passed Advanced Driving Test in March 1963 and became a member of the Institute of Advanced Motorists.
- Became a Driving Instructor for the Wessex School of Motoring in Ilford, Essex. Instructed for 32 hours per week from 1962 to 1964.
- Became Technical Representative for Automotive Refinishing Division of Major Paint Conglomorate. Average mileage 50,000 pa throughout UK.
- Designed, built and tested specialist sports cars for four years.
- Joined Aston Martin Lagonda Ltd by invitation as Paint Consultant and Quality Control Manager. Test drove every Aston Martin and Lagonda built from 1983 to 1991. This included high speed testing of all models including the Zagato Coupes and testing in the USA from AML Works in Connecticut.
- Instructed by Aston Martin Lagonda Ltd to evaluate the 'Drive and Survive' course at Ford Motorsport, Boreham circuit, for future training of Aston Martin test drivers.
- Now drives 30,000 miles p.a. as a paint consultant involved with business using Aerospace Technology in vehicle paint systems.
- Driving experience in the UK, Europe and the USA.
- Now driven over 2 million miles in total.

INTRODUCTION

I believe that knowledge gained from experience should be passed on from one generation to the next. It really is the way that a civilised society makes progress towards a better, safer world, in which everyone benefits.

Sadly, people are killed and injured every day on our roads. This book is my small contribution to try and reduce those numbers of personal tragedies.

Too often individuals find out the hard way, usually at the cost to others as well as themselves, and repeat the mistakes made previously. Attempts must be made to break this endless cycle of events.

I hope that my experience and observations noted over forty years and over two million miles of motoring will help drivers of all ages and experience to improve their standards so making the roads safer for us all.

I have also used my flying experiences as a pilot to demonstrate how I believe a more thoughtful and professional approach can be made to safer driving. I have included some reflections and experiences from my many years at Aston Martin Lagonda Ltd., when I test-drove every new car that was produced.

I hope this book is informative, memorable and amusing. I also hope that it will make a small and real contribution to road safety.

Peter Child, June 2001

CONTENTS

THE BASICS

There are just a few good basics to safe driving for a competent driver. The list is as follows:

D - Driver and vehicle in good condition
A - Awareness and road reading
D - Distance between vehicles
L - Lane changing and overtaking
A - Atmosphere and the weather conditions
D - Density of traffic

Always remember **DADLAD** and everything else is a variation on the theme.

DRIVER AND VEHICLE IN GOOD CONDITION

The Driver:
- Fit and well with eyesight checked. *(There is no formal eye test for driver, other than peering at a number plate that the examiner thinks is about 20 metres away. This is a very large loophole in checking driver safety. Many drivers require glasses for driving with emphasis on night sight. 68% of accidents happen at night. Please get your sight checked.)*

- The driver must not be tired and certainly have taken no drink or drugs. *(Remember that you, as a driver, are in command of a vehicle that may weigh as much as two tonnes travelling up to 70 mph legally. The forces involved are tremendous. Hit anything and serious consequences result every time.)*

The Vehicle:

- Ensure that insurance, car tax and MOT are current.
- Ensure that it has been correctly serviced.
- Daily walkround check should be:
  tyres in good condition and correct pressure.
  lights clean undamaged and working
  indicators clean undamaged and working
  wipers clean undamaged and working
  washers working.
- Seat set comfortably and adjusted correctly and not too near the steering wheel. *(This is because there needs to be a safe and clear distance for the air bag to deploy without harming the driver.)*
- Safety belts all working correctly.
- Windows clean for good view in all directions.
- Check the brakes are in good working order by touching the brake pedal as you first move off.

AWARENESS

Be aware of hazards ahead and learn quickly to identify them. Cars pulling out of side streets, pedestrians near a zebra crossing, people getting off a bus.

Be aware of your distances, closing on stationary traffic, approaching traffic lights, keeping the correct safe gap between you and the car in front. Always remember to watch the nut behind the wheel of the car behind the one in front – yes you!

Be aware of developing situations, several things normally need to take place to result in a road traffic accident. If you can spot situations as they begin to go wrong then an accident can be averted. Other people may be saved because you are practising good driver techniques.

Be aware of vehicle speed, especially at night. If you are not constantly monitoring your speedo you can have a shock when you glance down and see the needle hovering around 70, when you thought you were doing 50 mph.

Be aware of changes in road conditions, the surface may change, or as night draws on dampness may cause a slippery surface.

Be aware of the weather at all times, especially if it changes very quickly and with little warning.

DISTANCE

So many accidents are caused by motorists driving too close to the car in front. This is especially so on motorways. It only needs someone about five or six cars ahead to brake gently and as each car following brakes more fiercely to compensate for the thinking and reacting distance, the person in car six has nowhere to go except into the back of the car in front. I have witnessed so many `shunts` on the M1, M6 and M25 that I lost count many years ago. And it is so easily avoidable. Just stay back, and if someone overtakes on the inside to fill your safe braking space, then just drop back yet again. The time lost is miniscule within your overall journey time. That has been proved by all the motoring organisations.

If you do have an accident on the motorway then you can

be assured that you are going to be delayed for a very long time indeed.

Remember that your safe braking distance increases with speed so keep well back when you are motoring fast on the motorway.

LANE CHANGING

Be sure to check the road behind you and the blindspots on your car before doing anything. Indicate early and move slowly. Give plenty of space between vehicles. This gives all other motorists a chance to take some action if needed, and this can be done safely.

When overtaking on a single carriageway, make sure that once you have committed yourself to the manoeuvre you complete it as quickly as possible. Accelerate past the vehicle you are overtaking and move in without cutting the other motorist too short. Exposure time on the wrong side of the carriageway should be minimised.

ATMOSPHERE

Check the weather. Rain reduces visibility and increases safe braking distances. Snow and ice are very hazardous. Smooth driving is required so as not to induce a slide or a skid. Mist and fog cause reduced visibility and require extreme concentration to drive safely.

Drive on dipped headlights and with rear fogs on. I am amazed how many people do not do this and I notice they normally drive grey or silver cars, the perfect camouflage colours for fog. Road surfaces will invariably be wet when fog or mist are present, and often some icy patches will add to the difficulties. Be aware and you will not be caught out.

DENSITY OF TRAFFIC

As traffic density increases, then the chances of a collision will increase because of the nearness of so many vehicles in close proximity. Be aware of traffic flow and movements all round your vehicle. Watch everybody very closely, very closely indeed.

"..........not too near the steering wheel."

NOTE 1

PASS THE TEST – GOING SOLO

You have just passed your test and you are elated and may now drive solo. What is certain is that you will drive carefully and you will try and remember everything your instructor has taught you; therefore you are likely to commence your driving career in a satisfactory and safe manner. However, this normally does not last for long!

For a start, you have been driving at 30 mph for almost all of the time and you will become intoxicated by speed, the thrill of being in command and the adulation of friends and family. Note: this does not include any licence holder, normally a relative, who may have sat with you in the family car prior to your lessons at a driving school. Remember, they stalled and 'kangarooed' with you in the back streets of your hometown and are fondly known as the 'white knuckle brigade'.

In a short time of driving it seems the mist of uncertainty clears from your vision, and you now see everything as crystal clear and in sharp relief. It is now all so easy. To begin with you thought that with three pedals, only two feet and to operate them *and* to change gear at the same time - the whole thing was impossible! The list of seeming impossibilities went on and on, but now it's a piece of cake! Anyone can do it and you wonder what all the fuss was about.

This is the time when, sadly, many people have an

accident. After the event the same statements are made time after time.

'I didn't realise how fast I was going'
'I didn't see the other car until it was too late'
'I braked hard but was too close to stop in time'

Hopefully, only the vehicles are slightly damaged along with your pride. Sometimes it is more serious.

If you do have an accident, reflect on what caused the event. It is likely that if the inexperienced driver had driven in the manner taught by the instructor, they would not have been responsible for the incident. I believe accidents are avoidable and do not subscribe to the theory put forward by some that every driver will have an accident on regular time cycles.

In the early days of driving experience it is useful to re-live and think through every aspect of the journey. Be critical and think where you made mistakes or misjudgements, in closing distances between vehicles for example. Perhaps in a busy high street where pedestrians, old people or children attempted to cross the road without looking carefully. Ask yourself how soon you saw them, identify them as a hazard and take appropriate action by slowing the vehicle or braking.

When you observed a car in a side road about to pull out and join the traffic flow, did you believe that the vehicle would remain there and pull out after you had passed, or were you ready to slow down and brake if that driver misjudged your approach speed?

How accurate was your steering?

How smoothly did you change gear?

Did the car vibrate as you changed to a higher gear too soon?

If you stopped en route, how good was your parking? *(Remember, you can always practice parking and the way to overcome the fear of parking is to become good at it.)*

Major points to consider for safer driving are awareness and *smooth control* of your vehicle.

Your instructor will have told you to drive smoothly so that the car will:

- remain under good control
- last longer and give a higher mileage
- use less fuel so causing less pollution
- give you and your passengers a comfortable ride

Occasionally I was the passenger with a test driver, who was not employed by Aston Martin Lagonda Ltd, who was fondly known as 'Pants in the back'. This was because he screamed the engine in every gear giving maximum acceleration, so causing your underpants to arrive in the back seat without you removing them! He always braked to a standstill with 'G' Forces that would have given an RAF Tornado pilot some concern. He wrecked exactly the same number of cars he drove, including his own. It may have appeared macho but it was awful driving.

Awareness is a difficult thing to teach well because so often the routine of a regular journey, or the fact that some other concern is clouding your concentration, makes you less aware.

I have heard people say 'I came home from work last night and didn't remember a thing about the journey'. 'Oh, my God!' As the Americans say.

What actually happened?

The driver drove a familiar route and because of preoccupation was unaware of the circumstances of the journey. Had something untoward happened then it begs the question of how prepared was the driver to cope with an unexpected hazard?

Practice relaxing in the vehicle whilst raising your concentration levels, awareness and ability to predict likely scenarios in order to cope with them in ample time.

Reaction time is a very precious commodity and gets considerably less with the increase in road speeds. At higher speeds you have so little time to do much, and therefore you must anticipate events. Like flying safely, do not get into a position that you cannot get out of.

Try to read the road ahead in three stages:

    Distance
    Middle Distance
    Close

Look to the distance for road configuration, e.g., bends, traffic lights, oncoming vehicles overtaking and other hazards that might appear.

In the Middle Distance watch for hazards that have appeared, slowing or braking to counteract developing situations.

Close to, take avoiding action if totally unbelievable behaviour of other road users occurs, e.g., pulling out of a side turning without looking or even slowing, or an elderly person stepping off the pavement. It does happen.

It is important to make decisions quickly and responsibly. You are in command of your vehicle, no one else. You are alone, there is no instructor on board to take control and save you from disaster. Your decisions must be the right ones. This is where your training comes in, you are taught to control your vehicle and be aware. Forget the speed driving for the time being and concentrate on the basics while you gain valuable road experience.

There is no substitute for experience and the application of the knowledge gained from the experience to the matter in hand.

An example to contemplate - but only for a moment.

You are going on holiday to sunny Spain. You are given a choice of pilots to fly you. Either Captain Steadfast, suntanned with a touch of grey hair at the temples, who has flown the route for twenty years, knows all the radio beacons, compass headings, diversion airfields by heart, or Captain Whizzkid. He is just out of training, a very competent pilot, his aerobatics are really something to experience, navigation needs a little improvement, but he certainly will bring a new thrusting and dynamic approach to your journey to the sun. It will be his first flight to Spain.

No contest. Your fear of flying demands Captain Steadfast with all his experience.

In reality, Captain Whizzkid, after he has obtained his Commercial Pilots Licence, remains a co-pilot for many years before getting the chance to sit in the Captains seat, so he may continue training and build up his experience. So enjoy your holiday flight, it is and always will be the safest part of your journey.

Your experience counts, so learn by it. Listen to other drivers and learn by their experiences as well.

When you learn to fly many of the same principles apply. Your awareness is somewhat sharpened by your instructor teaching you that inattention to low air speed at low level may cause the aircraft to stall and you are likely to end up seriously dead. It concentrates the mind. As a result, pilots listen carefully to instructors and fellow pilots with more flying hours. Knowledge and experiences are passed on, remembered and thought about, and they will be a source of information and help to the less experienced. It is not necessary to keep repeating all the mistakes made by previous generations.

Learn by your experiences and the experiences of others. Observe other road users and identify good driving as well as the incidents of bad driving. Turn that experience into good, safe, enjoyable motoring and drive with humility.

SAFETY POINTS

- Remember as much as you can of what your instructor taught you.
- Be aware of what is happening all around you on the road.
- Learn by your experience and the experience of others.
- Always control your speed, things go wrong so fast at higher speeds.
- Pretend your car is brand new and straight out of the showroom.
- Try to relax in the car as you sharpen up your concentration.
- Only drive where you can clearly see.
- Concentrate on what you are doing.
- Behave reasonably.
- Remember Captain Steadfast.

NOTE 2

FIT TO DRIVE

When you apply for your driving licence you declare that you are fit and well enough to drive a car. Your examiner, at the time of your test will ask you to read a car number plate on a parked car at approximately 20.5 metres or 67.5 feet distance. I do not know how, if ever, this is measured by the examiner, but it is the only eye test that you will ever be required to have by law for the whole of your life. This, in a single word, is disgraceful. Everyone who drives should be required to undergo a proper sight test and some form of medical check at their G.P.'s surgery at pre determined times throughout their life. Contrast this state of affairs with a pilot. A full medical is required and this must be passed before being allowed to fly solo. The pilot is then required to pass a medical at very regular times until the pilot reaches the age of 50 when it becomes an annual affair. This is just for private pilots. commercial and military pilots have to pass a medical every six months.

At the very least have your eyes tested; it could save your life as well as someone else's. Poor night vision is an area where there is great concern. 68 per cent of accidents happen at night and I wonder how much poor eyesight plays a part in these accidents.

You must be fit and well to drive. Your alertness, awareness and concentration all fall to lower standards if you are unwell, and on today's roads with speeds and traffic density increasing you need all your faculties present to cope safely.

Tiredness is a killer and it is now becoming more apparent that many late night and early morning accidents are caused by drivers dozing at the wheel. The absence of skid marks before the impact is a clear sign to the traffic police investigating the accident that the driver was sleeping at the point of collision.

Take a break. Stop the car and get out and walk, drink coffee or alternatively have a good doze in the car after you have parked safely, away from the road, i.e., in a motorway service area. In a normal days driving you should stop every couple of hours for a complete break and to stretch your legs. Your passengers will thank you. Opening the window and turning up the volume of the radio is of very limited help.

Most important of all, DO NOT DRINK AND DRIVE. Alcohol slows everyone down and no matter how well you feel after a drink or two, your driving ability is impaired. Few people believe this but I can assure you it is true. Many years ago when you went for RAF Aircrew Selection, one of the tests was to sit in a small cockpit watching a cathode ray tube and by use of the control column, chase a white dot around the screen. You were timed whilst attempting to carry out certain manoeuvres in this exercise. The RAF carried out this test with two young fighter pilots sitting in two cockpit simulators. The first random test showed their reaction times to be within thousandths of a second. One of the pilots was then given half a pint of beer. The tests were repeated. The pilot who had drunk the beer was measurably slower in reaction time. The test continued until after a couple of pints there was a tremendous difference. These two young fighter pilots were 100 per cent fit and very highly trained. How do you think an unfit, overweight 40 something man or woman would cope with reaction tests, after a few drinks - very poorly is the correct answer. That is why you must not drink and drive. Just think, if you are caught over the limit your licence has gone for a year and possibly your job, if it entails driving. Insurance becomes difficult and expensive after you have your licence back, and that is the least of it. If you cause an accident you could be responsible for the death of another person, possibly even your own.

I often think this is why traffic police find it hard to have any sympathy at all with motorists who drink and drive and then go on to cause accidents. Always remember, the police are usually first on the scene of the accident, followed up by the paramedics in ambulances. They all witness at first hand the carnage caused by some stupid person who has been drinking. There are few things worse than hearing trapped, injured people screaming for help by the roadside. Ask any traffic policeman or paramedic. We all owe these very professional experts a great deal. Afterwards it is the policeman's job to go round to the victim's home and tell a husband, a wife, a mother, a father, a daughter or a son that their nearest and dearest is injured or dead. Not for the faint hearted. Give a kindly thought to the next policeman you see.

These days there are usually two or more cars per household, and it seems that everyone over the age of

17 is a driver. So, elect before you set off for the night who is going to drink and who is going to drive. The driver stays on soft drinks and the partner can let his or her hair down. This is the way to do it and it should be second nature in every home. If you both want to go mad at Nellie's third wedding, then get a taxi or stay the night. It is so easy.

A good thing to remember is the flying motto of "24 hours between bottle and throttle".

New legislation and test equipment are being brought forward for the roadside testing of motorists who may be under the influence of drugs. Not too soon at all, and the police should be given all the necessary powers they require to stop and prosecute drugged drivers who take to the roads. No one in their right mind wants any member of their family or friends projected into the life hereafter by some nut, high as a kite, attempting to drive a car. All this is about personal discipline. We must all have it so that we may all safely drive about our business. Let everyone try and be sensible and realise that so much grief can be easily avoided.

A rather important gentleman who owned an Aston Martin Lagonda spent too much time at his club bar, and consequently could not possibly drive home. The club was full so he was unable to stay there, and it was too late to book into a hotel. A taxi would have been the answer but that too was impractical as he lived over a hundred miles away. He staggered out to his parked Lagonda and unlocked the door. He returned to the club reception and gave the keys to the steward and said " I'm sleeping outside in my Lagonda, old chap, you keep the keys safely in here tonight and don't let anybody blurry well have them. I'll be back in the morning for coffee. Goodnight, old chap." He returned to the Lagonda and settled down across the back seat, allowing himself to sink into the soft 'Connolly' leather. In the early hours he was disturbed by two policemen walking their beat. After enquiries proved that he was not in possession of the car keys no further action was taken. How sensible.

SAFETY POINTS

- Be fit to drive and, if in doubt, have a medical.
- Get those eyes tested regularly.
- Check your night vision.
- Do not drive if you are tired.
- Do not drive if you are upset.
- If you are both up for Nellie's wedding then get a taxi or stay over. Think what can happen to you and your loved ones.
- Do not take drugs and drive.
- Do not drink and drive. JUST DON'T.
  Remember 24 hours between bottle and throttle.

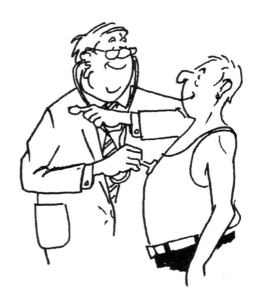

"Have a quick medical and eye test."

NOTE 3

SMOOTH DRIVING

Smooth driving at any speed will ensure that the car remains under good control and it is particularly important when driving in slippery or icy conditions. Smooth acceleration, steering and braking will minimise any sliding or skidding. Erratic handling in dry conditions will cause tyre wear, steering and brake wear and give passengers an uncomfortable ride.

Smooth driving becomes more important and critical to vehicle safety as the speed increases. At very high speed it becomes necessary to have very little input into the steering for the car to move, and all input must be extremely smooth.

Most passengers, what ever their age, sex or relationship with the driver wish to have a magic carpet ride. In comparison travelling with an erratic driver is like sitting on the back of a limping camel. Most travel sickness may well be caused by poor driving. In the fume free, well stabilised car of today, these influences that caused passengers to feel unwell, no longer exist.

As the world population is being urged to be 'greener' to stop the 'greenhouse effect' the use of fossil fuels comes under even closer scrutiny. With the trend going towards low sulphur petrol and diesel. If every driver accelerated smoothly from the traffic lights instead of practising Formula One Grand Prix starts the lesser fuel burnt would make a contribution to cleaner air. Heavy and sustained acceleration practice in any car, no matter how economic, will increase fuel consumption dramatically.

Erratic driving will cause unnecessary wear on all the vehicles moving parts, with special emphasis on tyres, steering, brakes and suspension. Cars are expensive enough to run without increased repair bills that are quite unnecessary.

Smooth control of the car will ensure that if you unexpectedly hit a patch of slippery road caused by ice or fuel spillage, you are unlikely to slide out of control into the nearest ditch or worse, oncoming traffic.

Smooth braking will give better control early on in the manoeuvre and bring down the speed progressively as the momentum reduces. If you are braking to a full stop, such as traffic lights, early smooth braking will mean you will stop without being a hazard to following traffic, and you and your passengers are not pushed forward into the windscreen. And the brakes last longer! As you come to a full stop just ease off the brake pedal at the very last moment. This will stop the car from an uncomfortable final jerk.

By steering smoothly through bends and corners the car will respond to your careful driving and it will replicate the smoothness that you put in with a balanced ride. At higher speeds this is very important when a speed momentum develops and very good time can be achieved on the journey.

As you change gear, hesitate momentarily as you pass through the neutral gate. This enables the syncromesh time to align a little closer and save wear and tear in the gearbox as well as giving you a better ride and the transmission smooth power delivery to the driving wheels.

When attempting a three-point turn or reversing into an opening do make sure the car is standing still before selecting reverse gear. I have seen drivers who should have known better, push the gearstick into reverse with a horrid clunk, as the car is still moving forward. The load through every part of the transmission is enormous.

Smooth car control, I believe, saved me from a difficult situation in the early hours of one morning going north on the M1 motorway. I was coming to the end of a long test drive in an Aston Martin Zagato and had just passed the Junction 14 turn to Newport Pagnell. I had planned to run up to Junction 15 at Northampton and turn there for the home run to the Works in Newport Pagnell. I had positioned the car in the centre lane of a totally empty motorway. The night was dry and very clear with excellent visibility. The Aston was performing beautifully as usual and everything was running smoothly. I started to notice little twinkles on the road surface and they suddenly became more numerous as I progressed. I realised that there was a frost on the road and at the same time the Aston began to slide very slowly towards the centre crash barrier. I attempted to steer smoothly back into the centre lane but it was to no avail. I was simply going too fast for the sudden change in road conditions. I kept the steering wheel as still as I could and *very* gently eased my foot off the accelerator. This movement had to be done ultra smoothly as a manual car with the enormous power of an Aston Martin Zagato would react on a slippery surface if a sudden reduction of power was to take place. It seemed an age as the speed of the car slowly subsided and the slide towards the barrier became less. I was finally able to ease the Aston back into the centre lane where I carried on reducing the speed down to 50 mph and I the moved into the slow lane. I returned to the Works at Newport Pagnell very chastened indeed by the experience. The Royal owner was due to take delivery of his car within days of my test drive. It would have been a major disaster if I had damaged this hand built bespoke vehicle because of my inability to read the change of road surface at speed. Smoothness saved me.

SAFETY POINTS AND CONSIDERATIONS

- Drive smoothly at all times.
- Make it smoother the faster you go.
- Erratic driving can cause loss of control.
- Smooth driving keeps good control, especially when unexpected hazards occur such as frost or ice.
- Smooth driving saves fuel and helps the planet.
- Smooth driving makes happy passengers.
- Smooth early braking helps other drivers as well as your passengers.
- Hesitate when changing gear for a smooth operation and less wear in the gearbox.
- Smooth steering helps to lessen wear and tear.
- Stop the car before engaging reverse gear.

NOTE 4

PASSENGER CARE

When you learn to fly you are given a little booklet and instructions on how to take care of your passengers. It would be an excellent idea if similar information were provided for drivers.

Passengers comfort and safety are very important. A good driver wants to give a smooth, comfortable and safe ride to passengers. If the driver fails to do this there is a serious downside, passenger discomfort can be both unsettling and distracting to the driver.

Start off on the right foot. Plan the journey and think of the requirements of the people you are carrying. Agree with your passengers as to where you intend to stop for comfort, tea and coffee breaks. That helps to allay any anxiety they may have. Let them know that according to the Radio, the AA or the RAC the route is free of holdups or roadworks at the moment and you expect a smooth run through. Remember your holiday flight when the Captain said " Ladies and Gentlemen this is your Captain speaking. We are at thirty thousand feet and our speed is 500 miles an hour. The weather ahead is very good and settled and our estimated time of arrival at Malaga is in an hours time at four thirty. We will have a smooth descent all the way in." You feel all cosy and lovely because you know that the man at the controls is in full command and the trip will be sunny, smooth and warm. Try and make your passengers feel the same. Small measures will ensure confidence in your passengers and make them feel better about the journey. Most people have some apprehension about a trip, especially if it is going to be a long one. Show them the map and explain your route and where you intend to stop.

Make sure the car is:

- clean inside
- checked out on oil, coolant and washer levels
- fuelled up

It is surprising how many motorists set off unchecked and they spend considerable time looking for fuel, which can be unsettling for passengers.

Keep your journey time short between breaks. You know that children particularly will ask 'are we there yet?', when you have only been driving for a few miles. If a journey time is too long then inevitably tensions build. It is important to take the stress out of carrying passengers, there is plenty of outside road stress to occupy the driver's mind and any further internal distraction is unwelcome.

SAFETY POINTS AND CONSIDERATIONS

When you are ready to depart make sure that:

- Everyone on board is wearing a correctly fitting seat belt. *The law requires that all passengers are seated and wearing a seat belt.*
- Everyone is comfortable.
- Tell everyone that you will adjust heating and

ventilation to suit them.

- Any sweets, drinks or food can be easily reached.
- Radio, tapes and discs are to everyone's taste. Not always possible!

"'Spending time looking for fuel can be unsettling for passengers."

NOTE 5

ROAD CONDITIONS

The only contact the car has with the road surface is the four tyre imprints. On average each of these are about the same area as the sole of a man's shoe. Makes you think for a moment doesn't it?

Your car is driving, steering and braking through a very small surface area in contact with the road. Hence, slippery conditions or poor road surface can easily make that contact less than adequate for what you may have in mind. Skids, slides, loss of control now come a lot closer to home. Upset the balance of the car and those four tyre imprints are working very hard to ensure that you and your vehicle do not make a sudden exit to the left hand ditch. Tyre technology has advanced and is desperately important because that is the only contact that you have, and the tyres must take a work load which is quite remarkable. From high speed and continuous motorway driving to country lanes full of potholes, the tyre has to cope with the lot in all weathers.

The road conditions play a big part in car control and therefore road safety. During every motoring trip you will experience many different types of surface which all will have a part to play in how well the car remains in good and safe control.

Some older concrete surfaces are ridged and will cause 'rumble' as well as tyre vibration. This can happen at various speed ranges and can be off-putting to the unwary driver.

Very smooth tarmac surfaces appear to become greasy and very slippery after a light shower. This is because there is a film of oil, petrol and unburnt diesel contaminates lying on the surface. This is another situation where the tyres have to work hard to obtain the grip you need for safe driving.

The weather has dramatic effects on the surface and frosts will break up a tarmac surface and cause lumps to break away causing further disturbance to the smooth running of the tyres.

Breaking distances will vary depending on whether the road surface is wet or dry as well as its actual surface materials.

Country roads are often pot holed and broken away at the edges. This is cause for concern. As you move to the left to give clearance to oncoming vehicles, wheels can disappear unceremoniously down some pretty awful holes, this may cause cutting and other damage to the inside of the tyre. At the first available moment ensure you check for damage. Do not hesitate to take the car to a tyre fitting company for their experts to carry out an inspection.

Often the camber of the road is variable and can be a problem because of the unsettling nature as it is fed back through the steering to the driver.

NOTE 6

WEATHER CONDITIONS

The one thing that we all talk about in this country is the weather. It is forever the topic of conversation, but when it comes to driving, so many drivers seem oblivious to it.

Every aspect of the weather has some effect on a car and the occupants. The heart of the matter is whether a driver is able to understand what is going on outside the warm metal cocoon that is being driven down the road.

It is a top requirement when driving to think and be aware. It is the same with speed limits. A thirty-mile an hour limit does not mean that it is always safe to drive at that limit. There may be occasions in poor visibility or passing a school at the end of the day when twenty or even fifteen miles per hour represent the safe speed. The same thoughts apply to the weather. If the rainfall is torrential and combined with squally winds it would be foolhardy to drive on a motorway at 70 mph with spray and gusting winds. So many people do so with dreadful results. Your awareness of the conditions should temper your judgement as a driver as to how fast you drive and how early you anticipate hazards that may occur.

a) The effects of rain.

Depending how hard it is raining, the hazard will vary. For instance, lashing rain with high wind should mean a considerable reduction in your planned speed. Visibility will be badly affected, tyre contact on the road surface will be lessened and aqua planning can take place if the tyres are worn or the tread depth does not allow the water to be dispersed quickly enough. Skidding or sliding may result in the event of a sudden steering or braking manoeuvre.

Light rain after a dry spell will always leave the road surface greasy and slippery. These two extremes hold hazards for the unwary, and combined with poor visibility can cause dangerous situations. Always remember to put your dipped headlights on so that you may be seen clearly by other road users. In accident reports so many drivers state that they never saw the other vehicle. Be seen. The motorcyclists are absolutely right to ride their bikes with the lights on. For safety everyone on the road must be seen.

b) Effects of snow.

If you do have to drive in the snow, then make sure you are prepared mentally and physically. Your attitude to the driving and the problems that may occur will ensure that your necessary journey is completed safely. Physically be alert and make sure that you are carrying a shovel, blankets, hot drinks, food and a mobile telephone.

Only drive if you absolutely have to. Depending on the snow fall rate, and remember it goes all the way to the ground, decisions on speed and distance must be thought out. If the snow is turning to slush as it hits the road surface then this will allow a slightly higher speed than if it is lying on the surface and compacting down. Normally the road gritters have been out when there is likelihood of snow but sometimes with the vagaries of temperature change and the suddenness that we often experience in this country, you may well find yourself driving on un-treated roads. Smooth driving is essential in snow and if the vehicle begins to slide or skid then the best rule is to ease off the accelerator and steer the car in to the direction of the skid. Vehicles will respond rapidly to this, and providing you react quickly, unpleasant occurrences can be avoided.

At night in snow conditions, drivers often become mesmerised by the snowflakes coming towards them in the headlight beams. A driver can become very tired quite quickly so be aware of that. It is better to stop and rest rather than push on in the hope that things will improve. If you do break down or get stuck in a drift, then stay in the car, wrap up warm, telephone for assistance and stay put. You can run the engine for warmth but be careful that the exhaust is clear of snow otherwise you can be overcome with the exhaust fumes.

c) Effects of slush.

The danger here is if there are frozen patches under the slush. These can cause you to slide as well as de-stabilise the tyre pattern on the surface. Generally, provided that the car is being driven smoothly and at the correct speed for the conditions, then the journey should be accomplished safely. If the slush is heavy, then slow down to prevent build up under the tyres. Keep a good distance from the car in front. Braking distances quoted for normal conditions do not apply.

d) Effects of fog.

Visibility is the obvious hazard in foggy or misty conditions. Speed must be reduced drastically in these conditions. Some fog and mist conditions are made even more dangerous when the fog is patchy. One moment you may be able to see a reasonable distance and the next moment be plunged into a zero visibility situation. This is when the collisions occur.

The motorist in front has hit the area and is braking hard, then you follow and brake as his brakelights come into view and vehicles behind you have to brake harder to make up for their reaction time. Eventually unless everyone is well spaced back and anticipating the braking traffic in front, there is a collision. It is a question of being seen as well as seeing and it is essential that you put your fog lights on when in these dangerous conditions. Many motorists will not do it and I wonder why, perhaps they think they are running up an electricity bill at home.

Watch an air liner coming into land any night and it looks like a flying Christmas tree, this is so the aircraft can be seen, and remember the aircraft is also on radar and being controlled all the way in to a safe landing. When foggy conditions become so bad that they go below minimum levels set by the aviation authorities, the aircraft are diverted to another airfield. In other words, they do not compromise safety for one moment. If only motorists did the same. Do not drive in fog unless your journey is absolutely necessary. Do remember to switch off your high intensity fog lights as soon as the fog has cleared, otherwise you will be dazzling the following driver.

e) Effects of the sun.

There are two major effects of the sun that affect the motorist. First, when the sun is low on the horizon and you are driving into it: unless wearing suitable sunglasses and have the sun visors in the correct position, then obviously the driver's vision will be impaired to a degree depending on the brightness of the sun. Secondly, when the sun is behind you, then reflection of the brightwork of cars both in front of you and cars travelling in the opposite direction will 'flash' blind you momentarily. This can be dangerous, as your vision is again impaired and constant flashing into your eyes is not to be recommended. Suitable sunglasses are the answer, but if you find this still too much to cope with, then stop somewhere safely and take a break. Eventually the sun will either set or rise further, so making it safer for you to proceed.

Be aware that when the sun is low on the horizon and shining into the car from either side depending on your direction, then trees or bushes along the roadside can cause a flickering within the car. This can be very disorientating as well as distracting. Move your sun blinds to the side as soon as you safely can.

f) Effects of temperature change.

The changeable weather that we enjoy in Britain, as well as giving us something to talk about, brings a hazard in its own right. A sudden temperature drop at night can turn a damp road into one with icy patches.

This can be very hazardous for the unwary. A dry road can become very slippery after the lightest of rain shower, whilst a heavy downpour can cause standing water, which can result in aquaplaning. All these factors need to be recognised when driving. It just needs a little thought by the driver to ensure that speed is adjusted to suit the prevailing conditions which can, and will, change at any moment. Always be aware.

".......make sure you are prepared."

NOTE 7

NIGHT DRIVING

At night everything changes. As a pilot with a full licence you may have flown hundreds of hours in daylight, but you are not allowed to fly at night until you have been trained and hold a night rating. It is that important. 68 per cent of road accidents happen at night. Good drivers are aware of the extra hazards that nightfall brings and prepare themselves for it.

The first thing is to ensure that your night vision is up to standard, so do not hesitate to see an optician if you have any doubt. Many people suffer with night vision defects and a quick check will put your mind at rest.

Before setting off at night, do check the car out. Ensure all your lights are working OK and that the lenses are clean from mud or road film. Check the windscreen wipers and washers as well as all the windows of the car. Make sure you can see clearly.

Now for the tricky bit, the driving!

At night speed is deceptive, and if you have been travelling for some while on a motorway or dual carriageway, you will perceive your speed to be within reason, but a glance down at your speedo will surprise you. It is more than likely that your road speed has crept slowly up to something well in excess of what you thought. Modern cars are quiet, warm and comfortable and they will all waft you up gently to higher speeds without the driver noticing. As the momentum builds up and the vehicle settles down to cruise, then an increase in speed will surely follow. You may be driving late at night when there is little traffic and the next thing you may be aware of is flashing blue lights in your rear view mirror. You have been warned. The speed limit is 70 mph and whatever you may think about that, it is the law. There have been moves to try and raise the limit to 80 or even 85 mph and the police know that modern vehicles with good road handling and better braking systems can cope with these higher speeds, but the government seems reluctant to allow any increase at present, and the law is the law.

Night driving calls for better judgement of speed and distance. There are now warning signs and rumble strips at the end of dual carriageways or motorways as you approach the roundabout or road narrowing. These are there to make you aware of the change in road status as well as the hazard of the roundabout. At night it is so much harder to judge the braking distance and that is why the speedo must be constantly monitored. So many motorists end up in the middle of the roundabout because they were travelling too fast, even for the modern brake system to cope with.

On single carriageways the danger is when you or an oncoming motorist attempts to overtake a slower vehicle. It is extremely difficult to judge closing speeds at night with only oncoming headlights to gauge the speed. This is a very hazardous occupation and the best advice is to ensure that nothing is coming in the opposite direction before you overtake. It is worth waiting because you will only save a few minutes in the overall journey time and the risk really is not worth it.

Pedestrians and cyclists can be a real problem at night, especially if it is after the pubs or clubs have turned out. People will stagger out unexpectedly and cyclists can wobble out, and a good driver must be prepared for these things to happen. It is just so much harder to see them in time in the dark. Give everybody and everything a wide berth at night, and do that as safely as you can.

Watch for unlit obstructions. There is always one.

I was test driving an Aston Martin Zagato in the early hours and was travelling on the designated test route down the A5 towards Milton Keynes, when as I came over the brow of a hill to the north of Towcester. I suddenly saw a 25 litre oil can in the road before me. I braked heavily and almost stopped before I hit it. Luckily it was made of plastic and empty and therefore did not damage the Aston. It was jammed just under the front air dam and I managed to retrieve it without damage. It made me think. Even with the massive power of the brakes and the two tonne plus weight of the car, I was still unable to stop in time. And I thought I was good. I am now humble and careful going over the brows of hills or round bends at anytime where I cannot see the road clearly ahead.

When driving at night just be aware of the hazards. If you are prepared then you will enjoy a safe drive and often a pleasant one, as there is usually less traffic on the road.

NOTE 8

FAST DRIVING

This is difficult. The exhilaration of driving a car fast is an experience that every driver knows and enjoys. The skill required to do this safely is enormous. If things go wrong, then they go wrong very quickly indeed and the whole art of driving fast is simply not to get into a situation that you cannot get out of.

Having said all that, there is still much pleasure and enjoyment in driving fast cross country, and this can be done *safely* and *within the speed limits*. Good journey times with good progress throughout is rewarding as well as exhilarating.

It requires the driver to be fit and alert, the vehicle to be in tip top condition and the route to be clear and free flowing. To drive safely at speed requires good training and awareness. If the speed bug has bitten a driver deeply, then the best advice is to take up motor racing and enjoy fast driving under controlled and safe conditions.

To drive fast in this country now is difficult because of two restraining factors. The first is the sheer volume of traffic on the roads, and secondly, the mix of traffic. With the motorways such as the M25 and the southern end of the M1 almost at a crawl each and every day, it is just not possible to drive fast. The poor mix of drivers is when motorists who drive slowly or not often get caught up with businessmen or 'reps' hurrying around this congested island. At certain times, such as holidays, you see this mis-match coming together in more ways than one.

If a driver can afford it, then sound advice is to attend one of the many advanced driving courses that are available. I have attended one and it was an excellent training course that took in both road and race circuit driving. If it is not possible to go on a course then some of the following thoughts may help a driver to slowly gather the expertise necessary to maintain high speed safely.

To drive fast for any period of time requires great concentration and awareness. Distractions, such as chatty passengers or blaring music from the tape deck can, and will, cause the driver to lower their concentration levels.

Attempting to drive fast too soon after passing the driving test is another area of concern. Every driver needs time and experience to develop the skills necessary. After every journey recap on what happened and how you coped with it. Be critical of your driving. Ask yourself questions about your braking distances, did you move in too quickly after overtaking another car, did you notice that elderly pedestrian about to cross the road? What could you have done better on that journey? Self evaluation is something pilots are trained to carry out, and it works for drivers as well.

When I first had to test drive Aston Martin cars I went to the chief test driver, Pip Aries, and asked him to teach me how to drive the car. He said to me "That's about the most sensible thing you'll ever ask as a manager! Come with me." In my career, I had driven quite a lot of fast cars, but the Aston Martin in comparison was an uncaged tiger. Pip taught me a great deal, but one particularly good piece of advice was "At first you will probably only be able to drive an Aston to about 60% of its capability. Get your handling experience by test-driving on the same route so that you will know where there are hazards and difficult areas and then slowly build your speed up. In five years time you may be able to drive an Aston to 80% of its capability." The facts are that after many years testing night and day, I believe that I could only handle the car safely to about 75% of its capability.

To drive fast and safely you have got to be very good, very good indeed. And it does not happen overnight. It takes any driver time to work up their ability to drive any car to its maximum capability. There will be a limit to what you will be able to cope with. A test driver, who in my opinion was very good, confided in me that driving down the Mulsanne straight at Le Mans at just over 200 mph was his happy limit. He said that the bend at the end of the straight seems to come at you strangely fast! We all have our limits, be ready to recognise them.

A German customer purchased a new Aston Martin Vantage and after a short while he requested the service department if there was any further tuning that could be fitted to the car. Service advised him that at the time there were Stage One, Two and Three available on the Vantage. " Good" he said "I'll have Stage Three fitted" Service advised him to start with Stage One and then upgrade as he became used to the extra power available. The customer agreed and Stage One was duly fitted and tested. The Aston was returned to Germany and a follow up telephone call to the owner enquiring about the modifications carried out and his general satisfaction with the car caused him to reply " the Aston is very satisfactory and Stage Two and Three will not be necessary!" Quite right, the owner knew he had reached his limit!

Driving fast at night gives another dimension to the exercise. traffic density is greatly reduced and this eases the situation somewhat, but other hazards are distance viewing limited by headlight range and the difficulty other traffic may have in correctly assessing your closing speed, be they in your traffic stream or oncoming.

Choose times to drive fast, such as the early daylight hours at weekends or the time between 2 and 4 o'clock in morning, if the weather conditions are suitable.

SAFETY POINTS AND CONSIDERATIONS

- Develop driving skills daily and get good at the basics before attempting to develop fast driving.
- Be fit and alert.
- Ensure the car is tip top and suitable.
- Watch your braking distances – it takes so much longer to stop or even slow for a bend.
- Recognise your limits.
- Driving at night requires extra concentration.
- Do not be distracted by passengers or in-car entertainment.
- Be extra careful on routes unknown to you.
- Be aware of any known hazards or black spots.
- Do not get yourself into a situation you cannot get out

of.

- Drive very smoothly.
- Obey the speed limits and concentrate on 'flow' driving to make good time.
- Enjoy driving and get good at it.
- If you have a fright, then analyse what went wrong.
- Make sure all your driving actions are safe.

'Driving too fast after passing the test is an area of concern'

NOTE 9

MOTORWAY DRIVING

It is without doubt another failing of the driving test that no practical instruction is given for motorway driving. The fact that immediately after passing your test you are at liberty to head for the nearest motorway and proceed is really quite wrong. Officially, during your training and test you have never exceeded 30 mph. Whatever is in the transport authorities mind to allow such a situation is beyond comprehension.

The motorway should be the safest road you travel on because everyone is headed in the same direction with oncoming traffic separated by a crash barrier. However, your first time out on a busy motorway is a daunting experience and it would not be beyond the wit of man to devise some driving experience with an instructor at the end of tuition before the test date. This could be logged in a learner driver's logbook along with a number of set hours of night driving. This log could be presented to the examiner at the time of the test.

This is exactly what happens to pilots. There is a flying log into which every flight is entered, with various notes and comments. It is signed at appropriate times by an instructor.

This also brings up the point regarding relatives teaching people to drive. This is not advisable and only causes immense stress all round. A qualified driving instructor has been fully trained and the best advice is always to go to a reputable school of motoring for tuition. Professional training is vital to ensure that a learner becomes a good, safe motorist.

Driving on the motorway can be both boring or quite exhilarating depending on the amount of traffic and your approach to the experience. There are several basic points to remember at all times for your safe journey.

a) Keep a very safe distance from the vehicle in front. If a driver, just a few cars ahead, touches the brake pedal then all the following cars get closer and closer as their thinking and braking time uses up all the available space. The end result is a collision when vehicles run into one another.

If a motorist overtakes on the inside and pushes in front, then just drop back, because in the overall time of your journey you are talking about seconds lost. These precious seconds are not worth either road rage or an accident. Be content as you can be assured that there are more and more unmarked police cars on patrol with cameras watching for these motorists and the fines and punishments will get heavier as time goes on. Be assured that police patrols will pull motorists who are driving too close or 'tail gating' as it is called and again these motorists can be fined or worse for this offence.

Road Research tests show a difference between makes of vehicles in braking distances. During breaking tests at 50 mph a Range Rover took a further distance to come to a complete halt compared with a Porsche 911. Both are excellent vehicles but each is designed for different uses, one an unbreakable off-roader and the other a very fast, well-balanced sports car. The problem is that they and their owners are road users at the same time.

When travelling behind any vehicle leave plenty of space for braking in emergency, increase that space in the wet or poor visibility, and increase it further when driving behind high performance cars. Their design specification gives them incredible braking systems that a production saloon or off road vehicle will find hard to match.

b) On motorways always drive smoothly, and when changing lanes, move from one to another gently. This gives drivers around you plenty of time to adjust speeds if that becomes necessary to allow you to carry out the manoeuvre.

c) Always look carefully behind you and guage traffic speed before changing lanes and give plenty of indicator time. The more information you can give to other motorists the better and safer everyone will be.

d) When joining the motorway down the slip road, ensure that you accelerate and judge your joining point. This must be such that it does not cause other traffic, particularly lorries in the slow lane, to brake or swerve. Use all of the slip road. You will not turn into a pumpkin if you get to the end of it before joining the traffic stream. I have experienced motorists driving to the earliest point on the slip road to join the motorway and then stopping as if it were a major road ahead.

e) Once on the motorway, judge your speed to run with the traffic flow and only move lanes when you have settled down and had a good look at the traffic all around you.

f) Keep your lane discipline and when you move from the fast lane (centre lane) to the overtaking lane (outside lane) move back to the fast lane. So many drivers just get into the overtaking lane and stay there. I have witnessed on so many occasions a stream of cars in the overtaking lane with just a few dotted along in the fast lane and nothing in the slow lane. If every motorist would move over they would create a further 40 per cent of road space on the motorways. Well worth having.

g) As you proceed you are aware of the traffic in front of you but there is significant danger from behind when motorists may be misjudging your speed. Keep a constant watch in that rear view mirror.

h) If you have any form of mechanical failure then get to the hard shoulder as quickly and as safely as you can. Generally motorists will give you space to change lanes once they perceive that you have a problem. Summon help with your mobile or walk to the nearest telephone by the side of the motorway. When you return to your car to await help, it is advisable not to sit in it but to move up the embankment. Many accidents have been caused when vehicles have swerved onto the hard shoulder and collided with broken down vehicles.

i) If a lady driver is on her own then it is advisable to wait with the car until the police patrol arrives after her telephone call for assistance.

If the motorway is clear it is quite amazing how quickly a driver can get from one end of the country to the other. Modern cars and the motorway system has unlocked time and distance for everyone who drives. Enjoy this freedom and make sure you are safe.

NOTE 10

ROAD RAGE

This unpleasant phenomenon has now appeared and seems to be getting worse. Stress and impatience are the prime causes, and as the roads become more and more congested, the reported incidents of road rage will increase.

A recent survey showed that 3 out of 4 motorists had suffered road rage, and this seems to be caused by our inability to deal with strangers. Nearly all motorists believe that they are more than competent and all wonder why so many other drivers make bad mistakes.

Travelling is a nightmare and because of the lack of investment over many years we are all now suffering with cancellations on the railways, congestion on the roads and delays at the airports. This situation is not going to improve in the short term. It is important to realise this fact and relax. If we do not, collectively, take a more sanguine approach, then road rage incidents will escalate and road journeys will become even more of a nightmare. We are becoming angry at everything and everyone as our space is being compressed down by too many strangers; drivers will erupt when they observe some foolish act by another motorist.

Bad experiences at work or in the home can trigger off the final outburst on the drive to or from work. Another survey has shown that 4 out of 5 people are unhappy to some degree at work. This is because we all want and expect much more from life than it appears to offer us. Do not be fooled. The grass is not greener on the other side of the motorway. Unrealistic expectations of careers and personal involvements cause nothing but frustration, which then manifests itself in unpleasant ways.

All drivers need to take the pressure out of driving. I saw that very well demonstrated when driving through the West End of London with a client who owns a Rolls-Royce Camargue. This person is an elderly gentleman who has had a very long driving career and he showed great courtesy and consideration to all the drivers around us. He waited patiently at zebra crossings for pedestrians, all of whom waved or nodded at him. Taxi drivers slowed to allow this enormous Rolls-Royce to proceed and he waved his acknowledgement to them and so we progressed out of London onto the M40 where his courtesy and patience made our journey seem calm, totally effortless, very enjoyable and quick. Motoring should be like this and it is up to motorists to ensure that it is.

We have come to believe that aggression is the way to success. It is not, and only causes immense self-harm. No one likes an aggressive person, and few people admire them. So many of us believe we are quite nice but others, speaking truthfully, will tell us that we have all tended to become more aggressive.

Courtesy is the hallmark of good driving, but like many things today, courtesy seems to have been thrown out the window. Nevertheless, most motorists are reasonable and well behaved and although we still suffer too many road traffic accidents in Britain we are the most careful drivers in Europe and have the lowest accident rate.

Most drivers have at one time or another suffered from a road rage attack. This can range from the other driver shouting at you and making a rude two-finger gesture to stopping your car and giving some form of verbal or physical abuse. This is to be deplored and of course is a criminal offence if a person is physically assaulted.

There are ways of dealing with this unpleasantness. First, try to defuse the situation. If you have moved too close to another vehicle during an overtaking manoeuvre and you realise your fault as the offended driver gesticulates, then give a little wave to say sorry and smile and say 'sorry'. The other driver will lip read and an apology makes everything just that bit better. The other driver may still regard you as a hopeless case but at least you acknowledged your fault and apologised. The other driver will feel superior, and that is always good in lowering the temperature inside the car.

Secondly, eye contact is very important and you must judge whether it is right to look at the other driver or avert your gaze. If you acknowledge a faulty piece of driving then look at the driver and apologise but if someone has cut you up or pushed in at speed then do not engage in contact as that can soon escalate into a more serious situation.

At all times remain calm and keep taking the pressure out of the system. It works and can save unpleasant abuse and the upset that that may cause you. You may become unnerved and your driving for the rest of the journey may be of a lower standard because paramount in your mind is the uncouth yob in a car who was shouting at you.

If, in the final analysis, your car is stopped by a raving motorist, then when he gets out to remonstrate you can either reverse away and drive on to the nearest police station and report the incident or lock your doors and do not open your windows and let the other motorist have their say. Keep calm and smile a lot. If the driver becomes lunatic and violent you must protect yourself and get away as fast as you can. Get the car registration number if you are able and report the whole thing to the plice. There is nothing like the sight of a burly policeman on the door step wishing to make enquiries about a certain reported incident to calm down even the most violent 'road rager'.

Never put up with road rage. This is a civilised country so let us keep it that way.

Drive with courtesy. Believe me it will not slow you down, it just makes everything pleasant.

"....say sorry and diffuse the situation."

NOTE 11

CONGESTION

Congestion is a very serious problem, and with the failure of the railways and country bus routes to give a full and integrated travel system, we are left with little alternative to getting about other than the use of our own cars.

The cost of motoring is high and although attempts are made by various organisations to reduce the cost of fuel, it seems that at present there is little hope of that. We pay a disproportionate amount of fuel duty compared with all other countries, but it seems that there will be little change from any government on this matter.

The future trends clearly show that as a car owning nation we will carry on driving, because we have no option. However, our cars will get smaller and will become more fuel efficient and greener. This is all to the good. However, the traffic congestion will undoubtedly get worse.

The congestion is there so we must learn to cope with it. The south east is particularly bad with the M25 being just about the most congested and the motorways feeding the M25, M1, M2, M3, M4 and M40 and other major A roads suffer desperately with rush hour hold ups made infinitely worse by accidents. The M6 around Birmingham is a daily nightmare whilst Manchester, Liverpool, Leeds, Newcastle, Glasgow and Edinburgh, all have their fair share of congestion.

Try to plan journeys out of the rush hour times. If that is not possible then drive calmly and listen to the radio or other in car entertainment. Be patient and lower your blood pressure. If you are caught up in congestion, check your map and see if you can navigate around the problem. I have found that just to keep moving is a relief even if you are going to put more miles on your journey. Keep sweets and a hot drink in the car. If you are stuck, it all helps. Just wait, you will eventually get there.

To give an idea of how bad congestion is in other parts of the world the following true story illustrates the point. A Japanese customer ordered his Aston Martin from the Main Dealer in Tokyo and in time duly took delivery of the car. The showroom was on a slight hill in a very busy area. The customer drove the car out into the traffic and joined the dreadful jam. He sat there for five hours, not moving, because of an earlier accident the whole area had gridlocked. The owner at last got out of the car and went back into the showroom and spoke to the sales manager. They reached an agreement. The Aston was then reversed back into the showroom for the night and the new owner went home on the Tokyo Underground.

POINTS TO AVOID CONGESTION

- Plan your journey out of rush hour times if possible.
- Keep an up-to-date map in the car with diversionary routes already mapped out.
- Once you are in a jam then plan to get out of it, in a cool and calm manner.
- If you are late for an appointment then use your mobile to let your contact know where you are and

what has happened, and make sure you are stationary when you place the call.

- Always keep sweets or fruit in the car, they can help.
- Tune into the radio. There is a great deal of help and advice from the BBC and other stations.
- Finally, just accept that congestion is with us and it will be some time in the future before things improve in this country. We are way behind with our road improvements, and the experts were warning about this avoidable situation years ago.

NOTE 12

ACCIDENTS

Accidents – let us avoid them! Let us strive to have an accident free zone throughout Britain. This is a very good idea because not only will it ensure that people are not injured but the cost savings are enormous. For instance, a road traffic accident where a person is injured and has to be taken to hospital costs, at present, about £100,000. This is the total cost of police officers at the scene plus all their follow up work, the paramedics and ambulance crews, the hospital staff, doctors and nurses and all their work. The list of professionals involved and all the caring work they do just to clear up the injury and mess from one accident, seems endless. Imagine if these accidents did not occur, think of the millions saved in the cost of the National Health Service.

It is a horrific fact that since the first person was killed in a road accident in 1898 over 20 million people have been killed worldwide. Drivers and passengers do not suffer fear of accidents in cars, but flying seems to bring out deep soul searching. If a Boeing 747 plunged to earth once a month in Britain there would be a total ban on flying. However, the country seems to accept that same number of people being killed on the roads. It really is a peculiar mindset, and it is because the fatalities are spread around the country that it has little impact except for the grieving relatives and friends.

There is going to be tougher legislation brought forward

to tackle un-caring and irresponsible motorists who cause death and destruction by their dreadful and dangerous driving. This is long overdue. The list of people killed by drivers who often receive nothing more severe than a heavy fine for their crime grows ever longer. This must stop. It is all to do with responsibility. As a driver you are responsible for the safe conduct of your vehicle, your own safety and that of any passengers you may carry as well as all other road users.

Speed is one of the major factors involved in accidents. Motorists will argue constantly that speed is not the problem, but the undeniable fact is, that it is. This is because drivers who speed are not as good as they think they are and you can't tell them ! Recent figures show that where speed cameras have been installed by the roadside, that accident rates have fallen by more than half, and for every one mile per hour reduction in speed equates to a 5 per cent drop in the accident rate. This is the proof that speeding drivers are just not up to handling vehicles at higher speeds and being able to cope with situations that might arise.

I have to say again if every driver who thinks he or she is that good, really is that good, there would be so few accidents that all our insurance premiums would be about ten pounds and we would not have an accident repair industry turning over millions of pounds annually repairing damaged vehicles. Without doubt there will be more and more roadside cameras installed to curb speeding motorists. We had all better get used to the idea of driving within speed limits or losing our licences. I am sure that speeding will become as sociably unacceptable as drinking and driving in due course.

The motoring public has been subjected for a considerable time to many television programmes demonstrating various makes of motor cars being driven by journalists and others on runways on aerodromes where the babble talk is of 0 to 60 in umpteen nano seconds with a top speed, governed down of course, to a hundred and something. The power of television is never to be underestimated, and as long as these 'Test Drivers??' carry on screaming up and down and spinning round and round the impressionable section of the motoring public will inevitably try to mimic these 'experts??'.

It is of course, perfectly alright to drive like this, provided that you drive down an aerodrome runway to go to work or collect the kids from school. The reality is when you switch off the television and the responsibility begins when you get into your car to drive to your destination. Do not be fooled by these professional television presenters who drive cars.

Spectating is a favourite pastime whether it be television or an accident by the roadside. When watching the television, however, the worst that can happen is you might sit on your crisps or spill a drop or two of drink. Slowing to spectate at an accident can and often does lead to a collision with the car in front who's driver is also eager to see the damage and general mayhem. Be very aware of what is going on around you and pay great attention to all the traffic at the scene of an accident. Do not be a spectator motorist because it can result in another accident and it is totally avoidable.

Statisticians will insist that you are 'bound' to have an accident because the figures show that to be the case. No one is 'bound' to have an accident as I reminded one very sure of himself person recently. All pilots are trained from day one to observe safety systems and carry out all operations with that one item as the most important and second to none. This is why flying is the safest form of travel. Ground crews carrying out regular and documented maintenance of aircraft and pilots and co-pilots do nothing but check systems and fly to destinations with safety procedures fully implemented.

Several friends who are commercial or military pilots have flown all their working lives without suffering a crash. It can be done. As for drivers, I know several who have completed high mileages without being involved in a road accident. I, at the time of going to print, have driven over 2 million miles in Britain, Europe and the USA without having an accident, and this mileage includes road testing of Aston Martin cars every day for many years. It can be done, so let us all do it. Remember, you are not 'bound' to have an accident. I believe that survival comes down to awareness, concentration and consideration.

Regrettably drivers do have accidents and many pages have been written on this subject. If you do not count the drunk drivers, the high-speed motorists and the downright careless you are left with lots of minor bumps and scrapes. These are surprisingly expensive to repair as the deployment of an air bag costs about £1,000 to reload and refit, and this is before the accident repair garage has begun to replace damaged panels or start re spraying. The cost of insurance will undoubtedly rise considerably in the coming years and the effect of that can be a reluctance of drivers to insure their cars. What ever you do, make sure you are covered by insurance. It is a serious offence not to be insured, and I have often wondered why insurance companies do not give the motorist a little windscreen sticker for cars stating the insurance cover dates and the policy number. This would allow quick verification at the scene of an accident by the police and all other interested parties. Not hard that one. They do it in France.

The figures for the end of year 2000 show that approximately 1,250,000 motorists have no insurance cover, and the cost to the insurance companies due these un-insured persons is put at £250 million. We should not be amused. Heavy penalties should be imposed on these people who disregard the law and cause loss and damage to other motorists because we have to pay in the end with higher premiums There is no excuse, and there never can be.

If you do have an accident then you must observe the following rules:

a) Stop immediately.

b) Call for help if anyone is injured. Ensure you tell the emergency services that this is the case. Give accurate and clear details to the operators and emergency services. They can and will respond that much quicker with the right equipment if they know what they may have to tackle. For example, if you are sandwiched in a ten car pile up on the motorway, then the emergency teams need to know.

c) If it is a little bump with minor damage, swap details of name, address, telephone number and insurance company.

d) Do not admit liability.

e) Stay calm and controlled at all times, even if you feel angry because it is obviously the other driver's fault.

f) Inform your nearest police station at the earliest opportunity. They may not attend a minor accident, so be prepared for that eventuality.

If ever you know of someone who has had an accident and has failed to stop or report it then you must try to persuade them to do so. The police investigation will eventually catch up with them. Just to give you an idea of how thorough the law enforcement agencies are, when I was at Aston Martin I was required by the FBI in America to supply small panels sprayed with primer and colour coats to be held in the forensic laboratory for accident investigations. These could be used to match up any flakes of paint left at the scene of an accident by a hit and run driver. The forensic team only requires a minute flake to identify the make of car. They hold samples for every known manufacturer. Be aware that all police authorities have this forensic science at their fingertips.

Drivers who have had an accident will generally agree that the situation developed very quickly and the impact happened very fast indeed. The normal response when a vehicle is coming at you on the wrong side of the road around a blind bend is to brake as hard as you can in an attempt to give the dangerous fool time to pullover to the right side of the road. Unfortunately there often is not enough time or road space. The accident then occurs.

Two vehicles hitting each other is disastrous at any speed, and consider always that it is the combined speed of the vehicles which is so damaging. If two cars are both travelling at 30 mph at the point of impact then it is the equivalent of hitting a stationary car at sixty. At 45 mph it is the equivalent of 90 mph. Although modern cars are very well designed and engineered, then no matter what has been built into the vehicle for the safe protection of the driver and passengers, the higher the speed at impact increases the risks of death and serious injury.

If you have done all you can to avoid hitting an oncoming vehicle, then, at the last moment, quickly steer your vehicle away from the impending crash. Take to the agriculture! Literally do just that, because you are likely to suffer less injury by driving off the road into a ditch or a hedge than colliding with the other vehicle. It may seem foolish, but it is quite surprising how many cars can run off the road and suffer surprisingly little serious damage. Paint and panel damage is inevitable, but you and your passengers may escape relatively lightly from a very serious situation. Do not hesitate to get out of the path of an oncoming vehicle if it is clear that you will crash into each other. It is the best chance you have at a very dangerous moment.

Drive safely and remember it is all avoidable.

"The police have forensic science at their fingertips."

NOTE 13

RECOVERY SERVICES

As motor vehicle technology has improved over the years the chances of any correctly serviced car letting you down by the side of the road is rare. This reliability has taken some considerable hazards out of motoring. In the distant past a breakdown of some sort was always half expected, especially on long journeys. In older vehicles there was a toolbox with some useful items to assist, should the worse case happen and motoring was a bit more of an adventure. Today, however, the motor manufacturers are producing cars that happily will drive well over a 100,000 miles without any major attention. Nevertheless, some breakdowns do occur and it is well to be prepared.

Most drivers today have a mobile telephone, which of course is invaluable. If your car does come to an unhappy halt then assistance is only a telephone call away. If you breakdown on a motorway it can be expensive to obtain suitable assistance or recovery. If you already belong to one of the motoring organisations, such as the RAC or AA then you can leave it in the hands of the professionals. There are many organisations who offer excellent recovery and 'get you home' services which are invaluable to your peace of mind. If you are regularly driving on motorways or covering large distances, then it makes good sense to belong to one of these organisations. It allows the driver to set out on the journey knowing that should anything go wrong then there is a team standing by who can sort the problems out.

It is important to recognise the driver's role here, and it is up to that person to check the vehicle and ensure all fluid and oil levels are correct as well as ensuring that there is ample fuel on board prior to departure. A few moments spent before setting off may make all the difference. So many motorists run low on oil, cooling fluid, water in the radiator, especially in the summer when setting off on holiday with the family.

If the car is in good order you are more than likely to have a routine trip without a breakdown.

NOTE 14

TIREDNESS

It is now becoming much more apparent that many accidents in the late afternoon and overnight are due to tiredness and fatigue. This is a very real danger because in the warm comfort of a modern car it is so easy to become drowsy and then to fall asleep. Many drivers have died as a result of falling asleep and the traffic police are able to show that this was the cause of the accident because there are no skid marks up to the point of collision. This means that the car, van or lorry ploughed into the obstacle, such as a motorway bridge without attempting to stop. This type of accident is devastating. The figures show that about 300 people a year are killed and many seriously injured because the driver fell asleep.

Every driver must plan their route, even if it is only in the mind. Plan to stop every couple of hours for a comfort break and a cup of coffee. If you begin to feel just a little drowsy then stop as soon as possible at a safe place. Either get some rest or get out of the car and have a complete break along with food or coffee. If you still feel too tired then just make plans to stay where you are. Better sleep in the car than lay out in the mortuary.

Just think what you are doing and plan ahead. Do not try and drive a long way after a hard day at work. Certainly do not drive if you have been drinking or taking medication. Try to avoid driving between midnight and six in the morning when our natural clock shows that we are all less alert.

Always be aware of what you are doing. You owe it to yourself, your family and other road users.

SAFETY POINTS

- Plan to stop every two hours for a comfort break.
- Have a drink of tea or coffee.
- If you feel drowsy stop immediately in a safe place.
- Do not attempt to drive long distances after a hard days work.
- Do not drive if you have been taking medication that might make you drowsy.
- Do not drive if you have been drinking.
- Avoid driving between midnight and six in the morning.
- If necessary stop in a safe place and have a good sleep in the car with the doors locked.

"When you are tired, stop and sleep in comfort"

NOTE 15

CAR FIRES

This is a very rare event but occasionally it does happen. Most fires are caused by the electrical system, but I have experience one where a plastic fuel line split and sprayed neat fuel onto the engine manifold. It was quickly extinguished and very little harm was done.

If you do experience a fire, it usually starts with a pungent smell of burning plastic or rubber. Stop immediately and shut off the engine and ignition. Leave the car as quickly and safely as you can. Only attempt to tackle the fire if it continues and still appears that it can easily be contained, either by smothering it with a blanket, if you can get to it, or by use of a fire extinguisher. Every car should carry an extinguisher and you are obliged to do so when travelling abroad. If the fire takes hold, then abandon it and get far away as possible before summoning help. It will not be long before the fuel tank explodes, so put some distance between you and the car.

NOTE 16

CAR PURCHASE

I have often been asked which is the best car to buy, and I always reply 'the one that suits you'. The reason is that we all have different motoring needs and obviously what is suitable for one person does not suit another. What ever your requirements are I can assure you that there is a motor manufacturer who has the very car for you. In today's world the motorist is spoilt for choice.

It is worth making a list to see what items are your priority. As an example, you may be a person who needs to drive just ten miles to work and there is no alternative transport. As you will only use the car for this purpose because your partner has a car which you normally go out in to socialise or go on holiday, then an inexpensive small, fuel efficient, easy to park little whizzer will do nicely. The road tax is now less for smaller engine cars.

You may be a driver who does some charity work and you require a hatchback or an estate car for carrying items, and as you occasionally have to deliver these items a hundred miles away, then perhaps a slightly larger car would suit you best.

You could be a self employed technician and your work takes you all round the country, in which case you probably require a larger car with extra comfort features as well as the ability to cover large distances quickly. And so on. List your needs and then see what fits. Do not make the mistake of purchasing a Hoffenshuffer Mark 3 because you always wanted one, and try to make it fit what you need in motoring terms. It never works.

If you have a purchase budget, then stay within it. If you have made the right choice for you then ensure that you buy a car as young as possible, with a full service history and carry on servicing it as required by the manufacturer. It really does stop a lot of heartache in the end.

It is best to buy from a reputable dealer because you are assured that there is no hire purchase outstanding, or that it has not been stolen. If you wish, you can always have an AA or RAC inspection before buying and this should give you extra peace of mind.

If you buy privately, then please be aware that you may be lucky and find a genuine bargain, such as an elderly lady owner, who has only driven 20 miles a week for the last three years etc., or Jim, he's always down at the 'Dog and Rabbit' and has got a real little shiner for you. There is no reason not to buy from Jim, but this is where you need to have an AA or RAC inspection and also check the ownership and registration details to make sure that it is not stolen. If it is, and is then recovered by the police, you would have to pursue the person who sold you the car for your money. That can be a bit of a job as he might be inside!

It is now possible to purchase cars on the internet. Although you may appear to be making savings on the UK price by buying your little beauty abroad, there may be some points to consider.

It appears that there is some reluctance from main dealers to show interest in you car if it has been supplied by a dealer in Europe when it comes to warranty and servicing. By European law there should be no problems but there appears to be a little gap that needs your careful attention before you rush forward on this. So check this out.

Many UK dealers, who are generously overstocked with vehicles may cut some very good deals for you, so stifle your natural shyness and request their very best offer to you. You may be pleasantly surprised. That Hoffenshuffer Mark 3 that has been in the showroom for some time might be sold at a super competitive price. Give your dealer a chance to compete with the internet. I have found that sometimes it is more beneficial to deal with a person, where you can build a contact into a good business relationship. Remember, motoring is not just at the point of sale, there is a whole 'ownership' programme that may go on for years. However, if you think you can improve on the dealer's best offer and proceed to the internet, do ensure that when the car is delivered to your door that it is the right specification, colour and trim. I do know that some people have not quite got what they ordered. Be aware.

Think about what you are doing and plan to buy the car that suits you. It is out there waiting.

Ms Elizabeth Taylor, the legendary film actress, spotted an Aston Martin in a dealership in Los Angeles. She sent her secretary in to purchase the car and it was duly delivered to her home. Only then did everyone discover that Ms Taylor did not have a licence to drive. A driving school from Los Angeles was contacted and an instructor appeared in pretty quick time. He found to his utter horror, the lovely Ms Taylor preparing to take lessons in her Aston Martin, which was not fitted with dual control. It was decided in the end that a chauffeur driven limousine should drive out first, followed by Ms Taylor and her instructor in the Aston Martin, and another of Ms Taylor's limousines would follow. Ms Taylor was quoted in the national press as saying ' I feel quite relaxed, because whatever I may hit, I own'.

"....the Hoffenshuffer MK3 – not really suitable."

NOTE 17

COMPANY REPRESENTATIVES

Much of the road traffic today is business orientated. So many companies have large sales teams headed up by harassed managers rushing around the country carrying on business. Certainly the introduction of computer based methods of sales and enquiries may have lessened the need to have salesmen in cars, but there are still a lot of them about.

There is one very large problem for sales teams, and that is time. They need to be round their customers for orders and queries in double quick time if they are to meet ever increasing sales targets. Hurried journeys under the pressure of time are not always the best. Generally, the sales boys are good drivers but they do have a high accident rate, and one can argue that that is because they are on the road so much that they must be more likely to be involved in these unpleasant incidents. However, it is true to say that if there was not so much pressure from the hierarchy within the company for better figures year on year, it is likely that the accident rate might decrease.

Some large conglomerates are now sending sales teams on advanced driving courses to improve standards, which is all to the good. Some sales people do not like driving particularly and I wonder if they should be doing the job out on the road. If you are going to spend hours on end driving every day, it is no good if you really do not like it. You may be, unconsciously of course, an accident waiting to happen.

This is a problem for senior management and should be addressed. Accidents can kill and injure staff as well as costing the taxpayer and the company a great deal of money. I often think that both people and organisations take motoring too lightly and do not pay enough attention to it. Remember, a commercial pilots only job is to fly the aircraft safely from airport A to airport B. A salesman has to drive from customer A to customer B and then do his job. This is a very different affair. The safe driving between customers is as important as the sale, because if the salesman crashes between customers that is it for the day, week or month.

I have met some sales persons who are more afraid of the sales manager than they are of an accident. The slight accident may come almost as a relief from the pressure. If you're a sales manager reading this please take note and take some action. Ease the pressure, because it does no one any good. Find alternatives to heavy workloads and high call rates, tired sales teams do not work well and efficiently.

NOTE 18

MOBILE TELEPHONES

Mobile telephones are just great. The first one I used was at Aston Martin when I was going out on test with a special car which had some new engine management systems in place and the early bench tests showed up some bugs in the system. I was handed a telephone which was fitted on top of a small suitcase and was told to ring in if I had a problem and could not make it back to the works at Newport Pagnell. The car was fine and I did not have to use it, until a later date and I am glad because the whole thing was quite enormous! Today the mobile is so compact and so versatile that no one should be without one. For all sorts of reasons, from car breakdowns to requested help if your personal safety is threatened.

The problem, however, is when you attempt to use this little marvel whilst driving. It is very dangerous and distracting. You must stop in a safe place before switching on to receive that important call from Tracey about clubbing tonight. I have seen all sorts of motorists struggling, and I mean struggling to keep control of their car whilst talking on the telephone.

Recently I watched with horror as I waited at a roundabout in Milton Keynes. A man driving a Jaguar saloon holding a mobile to his left ear with his right hand attempting to negotiate the roundabout. Halfway through this unsteady manouvre he let go of the steering wheel to change hands. I watched fascinated as the car wallowed around all over the road like a cow on roller skates. Eventually the driver managed to get the car sort of lined up and shot off down the road swaying as he accelerated. You would not imagine that a driver could get into such a muddle. If anything had gone wrong whilst he carried out this ludicrous and dangerous manoeuvre an accident would have happened. He had no proper control of the car.

If the Police spot you driving with a mobile clamped to your ear you can expect to be stopped.

Think what you are doing with this little wonder before attempting to drive whilst talking. You can go the hands free route, but there is still debate about the safety of that at the moment.

The mobile is great. Think and use it sensibly.

More and more vehicles are being fitted with satellite navigation aids and route guidance systems. These are excellent and most useful additions to the modern car, provided that they do not distract the driver from the very important task of driving the car safely. Any item inside the vehicle that requires the drivers attention is a DISTRACTION. Never forget that distractions contribute to collisions. Use these guidance systems correctly with the very minimum input from you. Stop the car in a safe place or ensure that you are standing still in a traffic jam before you look away from the road ahead for any length of time. There have been a number of accidents where the driver has been distracted by these systems or in-car entertainment, where momentarily attention is given to tuning the radio or placing a cassette or CD into the equipment. Be aware of what you are doing, and if travelling with a passenger get them to attend to these various functions. Regard them as a co-pilot. You watch the road ahead.

"A mobile 'phone turns your car into a cow on roller skates."

NOTE 19

BLINDSPOTS

Sit in your stationary car comfortably, look out and ask yourself what can you see? The road in front? Of course but is any of your view obscured? Do you have furry dice for example? If you do, then think about them. Do you really need them? Ask yourself 'how much of my view forward is obscured by these furry things?' Too much for safety - so do without them. Now look in your door mirrors. How much of the road can you see? Check if there is a blind spot because you may have a vehicle in that very blind spot as you begin to change lanes on a motorway. This is important, because what is really happening is that you are manoeuvring your car on the road believing that no other vehicle is close enough to interfere with your intentions. If the other motorist does not see you, then a collision is likely unless at the last moment either one of you takes rapid evasive action. Every car will have a number of difficult areas or blindspots, you must ensure that you are aware all these before setting off on your journey.

So often after the accident the driver says 'I didn't see the other car until he hit me'.

Be aware and look carefully.

NOTE 20

OBSTRUCTIONS

Obstructions fall into two categories, those inside the car and those outside the car.

Inside the car these obstructions can be anything from window stickers, furry dice or old tins of lemonade on the floor, which end up stuck behind the clutch or brake pedal. I knew a salesman who was without doubt the most untidy person ever, and on a clear day you could see the floor carpet in the car. One day he got a coke tin caught behind the clutch pedal and luckily we were able to stop before anything serious happened.

When carrying animals you must keep them under control, in some sort of travelling basket or behind bars in the back of an estate car. Once loose they can pose a threat and it has been known for them to get around the drivers feet, causing a serious distraction.

Look around your car and see if anything is in the way of you reaching all controls and operating them. Purses, wallets, handbags can all cause an obstruction or distraction to the driver. Remember there is no problem until something goes wrong or there is an emergency. You need clear access to every control system in the car.

Obstructions outside the car really come into a difficult area where they are not often observed until too late. A concrete bollard set nicely but firmly in the car park, which you reverse into. A series of high kerbstones set in a row along parking bays that may not be readily seen at night and you drive into as you move off. The damage these obstructions cause can be quite considerable. Watch for them and be aware.

NOTE 21

WEATHER TRAPPED

The weather in this country plays a significant part in our lives. Other countries seem to have a climate, but we experience 'the weather'.

It effects everything we enjoy, from sporting fixtures to garden fetes, picnics and barbeques. The weather can be good and it can be bad. When its bad its awful, and it certainly makes a large contribution to the dangers and hazards when driving. These difficult conditions exist, and therefore we must try to minimise their effect on our driving and road safety.

Check the weather forecast before setting out on a long journey. During the winter months, be prepared for just about everything. Sometimes the weather forecast on the television mentions just about everything imaginable and it is surprising the variance throughout this small island.

First off, check the car for lights, indicators, windscreen wipers and washers and check all oil and fluid levels plus the spare tyre. Take blankets, food, chocolate and hot drinks. (Plastic shovel!). Ensure that you have ample fuel and be aware of the conditions and expect everything that the weather forecast promised.

Rain followed by flooding is becoming the norm and it is worth pointing out that a third of all accidents happen in the rain. This shows that the combination of poor visibility and less grip and control on the road surface which contributes greatly to the hazards of driving. The way a good driver can minimalise these effects is to keep an extra safe distance between vehicles and to ensure that the wipers are working efficiently along with the demister. In poor visibility put your dipped headlights on, because you must be seen as well as seeing.

When you approach a flooded section of road you must decide if it is shallow enough for you to drive through. This can be observed by watching other vehicles, and if there is doubt in your mind, stop and turn round and retrace your route to find another way. If you decide to drive through a flooded section of road carry out the following procedure :

a) Stop the car at the waters edge.

b) Engage first gear and move forward slowly so as to disturb the water as little as possible. If you plunge in, the splash is likely to knock out the electrical system on the engine and you will stop.

c) Proceed slowly with the engine running fast and slip the clutch so you are going slowly. This will ensure that if the water level is higher than the exhaust pipe the engine pressure will blow the water away so allowing the engine to keep running. If water invades the exhaust system the engine will stop as it will be unable to 'breathe'

d) If the engine does stop because of splashing or invasion of the exhaust system, then keep the car in first gear or reverse if you feel it is getting too deep, take your foot of the clutch and turn the starter. The engine will not run but the starter will crank the engine over and very slowly the car will move forward under control and eventually out of the flooded area. Here you can get out and dry everything off. It need not be necessary to jump out of the car when the engine stops and start wading around in muddy water, attempting to push your car out. (The use of the starter motor will only work on manual cars. An automatic transmission will not respond in the same way.)

e) Once through the flood test your brakes to dry them out and keep doing this at low speed until you feel that the system is back working to its normal standard.

f) If you have been through deep water it is good advice to have your garage inspect your car thoroughly. It can save you a lot of future trouble.

Driving in the snow should be avoided if at all possible, but sometimes the weather changes so rapidly that there is no alternative than to proceed. Listen out on the radio for weather advice and if it looks as if things will get serious within your travelling time divert safely into a motorway service station or wayside café. It is better to be there all night than stuck in the snow and having to sleep in the car.

If you carry on and eventually disappear into a snow drift then the advice is to stay put. Get on the mobile and tell the emergency services what has happened to you, as well as the family at home. Wrap up in the blankets, eat the chocolate and enjoy the warm drink. If the temperature goes on falling then run the engine occasionally for warmth, but be aware that if the exhaust is covered with snow you may have fumes coming into the car. Then just wait for rescue. The emergency services will get you out for sure. Do not going wandering off in heavy snowfalls.

Driving in heavy outbursts of rain or hail can be dangerous because of lack of visibility. Slow down gently to allow following traffic to do the same, and if you judge the conditions to be too dangerous to proceed, then don't. Pull over and park up until the rain or hail subside, unless of course, you are on the motorway when you should slow right down. (Always remember, you can only stop on the hard-shoulder of a motorway in an emergency.)

Always be aware of road temperatures and the fact that they can plummet below freezing on certain stretches. Road test laboratories do have equipment that allows technicians to thermal map a road surface whilst driving along it. With this valuable information they can map out the likely danger spots on a route, and signs may be erected to warn the motorist of likely icing. This is a good step forward, and if you see such a sign telling you that icing is likely, then take very good notice of it. That information could stop you from experiencing an unexpected skid. You may believe the road is just wet, and it may be so for many miles, but there may be an area, low down, in a bend with trees or exposed to a sharp cross wind where ice has formed. To be forewarned is to be forearmed.

There is a system under test where blue flashing lights appear when the road surface temperature goes below 8 degrees centigrade and hopefully there will be more of these excellent warning lights installed on roads prone to ice patches.

Watch the weather and be aware of it.

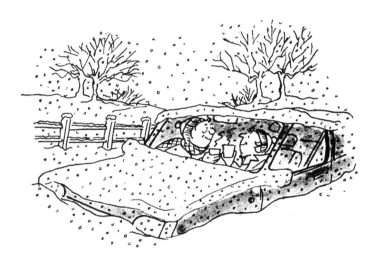

"When you're trapped, stay put and wrapped up."

NOTE 22

POOR ROADS

There has been considerable under investment in the road system for many years. Some people complain that more roads attract more traffic, but the truth is that if mores roads are not built the whole system will gridlock. The RAC have stated recently that the building of the M25 around London has reduced the heavy commercial traffic through London by 80 per cent.

Although the M25 is still too narrow in parts, down to two lanes in the north, it is still managing slowly to move heavy traffic volumes around London. A fact that all Londoners should be grateful for. We all require our cars to get about and we also demand fresh food in our local supermarket. Well, it can only get there by lorry. Customers today would not put up with food that was not fresh and wholesome. So think of the lorry driver doing his job to ensure you have got something good to eat for dinner.

Many 'A' roads are in poor condition with many accident blackspots. Although motorists are responsible for their actions, sometimes a major contributory cause is the road layout or lack of sufficient visibility for traffic joining a major road. When many of these roads were first built, traffic speed and density were much, much lower. Simply put, the road planners have not kept up with the motorcar. Governments have been reluctant to build roads for many diverse reasons and lobbyists seem to have been able to persuade everyone who would listen that road building is a 'bad thing'. It is a fact that in the case of the Newbury Bypass the protesters damaged many hundreds of trees (more than were to be cut down for the road). Check with the Forestry Commission on that one. It is important that we do not get hi-jacked by people's opinion rather than the facts.

Good traffic flow is the answer and if this can be accomplished, then traffic jams and hold-ups will undoubtedly reduce. The system on the M25 around Heathrow using variable speed control allows the authorities to vary speeds and monitor the flow of traffic. This is now working well and shows that such systems are beneficial to all. Most motorist would prefer, in congested areas, to be restricted to 40 or 50 mph provided that all the traffic keeps moving. Stop start motoring is bad news as it adds to frustration and pollution.

Minor roads, 'B' roads are either very good or very bad. I have driven on some that are wide, well surfaced with good visibility, and others that would cause concern to the driver of a horse and cart. It appears it is to do with money and the amount available to the county road engineers. It is all part of under investment.

To cope with the roads today, the good driver has got to plan the route, check the best time to travel and be aware of the hazards as the drive continues. Know where you are going and prepared to re route if necessary.

NOTE 23

LORRIES

Few car drivers appreciate the needs and concerns of the lorry driver. Some car drivers seem oblivious to these juggernauts as they pound along our road system. It is worth taking a few moments to outline some of their problems, so that car drivers can be a little more aware of what these giant road users require from the ordinary motorist.

The first thing to remember and always remember, is that they are unable to brake to a halt at the same rate as a car. It is important that the car driver does not move in front and slam on the brakes un-necessarily with a 38 tonne fully laden vehicle following. I witnessed this manoeuvre recently on the M1 at Junction 12 when a motorist pulled across to exit and very badly misjudged all the speeds and distances. The lorry driver, with great skill, managed to avoid the aforesaid chump. My hat goes off to you, sir, because I could see a major road crash developing in an instant. The motorist remains at large.

A lorry is required to keep up its momentum to reach preset destinations at certain times. It is a bit like an oil tanker at sea, it needs time to slow and stop and time to build up to speed. Car drivers can make it easier by keeping that fact in mind.

Lorry cabs are fitted with tachographs which gives the record of their journey times and speed. It also registers time that the vehicle stops for the driver to rest. What this tells you is that the lorry journeys are planned and work to routines.

Many lorries are owner-drivers. In other words, the driver is a one-man business with everything he owns going down the road. If his vehicle is off the road it is his livelihood, so ensure that if you are a car driver you give him a chance to stay in business. The less hassle he has to face each day the better he will be.

The police and various government agencies routinely stop commercial vehicles for all manner of checks on the vehicle, paperwork and axle weights. Road traffic police will tell you that many lorries belonging to big and small organisations are in pristine condition and a credit to their companies or owners. Some, however, let the side down, but generally we have a good commercial fleet in Britain.

Please be a good driver and give them the space they need.

NOTE 24

MOTORCYCLES

As traffic congestion increase more and more motorists are becoming bikers. It is an excellent way of getting about and really in the final analysis is the ultimate method of transporting a person. The only drawback is the weather in this country but with the modern biker leathers and protective gear it is less of a problem than it used to be. Motorbikes certainly use less fuel than a car and are virtually unaffected by traffic jams.

Car drivers must show courtesy and consideration to bikers because in the event of an accident the biker will suffer more injury than the motorist. It is an excellent idea that bikers keep their lights on at all times so that they may be seen by everyone.

Car drivers must be aware of the motorcyclists and ensure that they give them the space they need.

NOTE 25

HORSES

If you live in the country, then as a motorist you will be aware of riders and horses using the minor roads. In fact, you are likely to have grown up with them and regard them correctly as part of rural life. However, if you have lived all your life in a built up area or inner city you are unlikely to be aware of the needs of the horse and rider.

Dashing down winding country roads at speed can be great fun, but the fun can turn to disaster if you fly round a blind bend into horses being ridden along the road.

They have a proper right to be there and generally they will be under good control from their rider but will be moving slowly. A collision with a horse is a most dreadful experience. The animal can be so easily frightened and if it is injured in any way it is nothing short of a catastrophe. Be aware that you are likely to find horses on a country road and a good driver must ensure that :

a) You always drive at a speed around a blind bend that will enable you stop immediately if there is a horse and rider in the road.

b) You must wait behind the horse and rider before overtaking. Generally the rider will wave you forward when they are ready. It is the car drivers responsibility to ensure the road ahead is clear of oncoming traffic before overtaking.

c) Give the horse and rider a very wide berth and move well over to the other side of the road as you pass. The rider will always acknowledge your consideration with a 'thank you' and little wave.

d) If a horse and rider are oncoming then you should slow right down to a low speed crawl and allow the rider to ride past safely. The rider will thank you.

e) Sometimes you may come across a horse rider at dusk and they generally will have a light as well as some reflective clothing.   The   same   rules   apply. Acknowledge the wave.

Be aware of horses and riders in the country. They are an integral part of rural life.

"A salute for the good driver"

NOTE 26

TOWING

The number of motorists who tow is growing. With leisure activities such as boating, gliding and of course caravan touring increasing, then the need for a little understanding of what towing is all about must be welcomed.

Many organisations give extremely good advice on the technical side and it is well worth contacting an organisation that deals with your particular leisure activity. These notes are just general points to watch and be aware of.

Before even contemplating towing anything the driver must first ensure that the tow vehicle is of the correct weight and power to do the job safely and within the law. There are tables that set out the vehicle weight and the maximum weight that may be towed. Ensure that your vehicle and your luxury speedboat are right for one another. The penalties can be quite severe if you are all out of balance as well as the problems you may encounter whilst actually trying to tow the 'Skylark' to Southampton.

There are speed restrictions that must be observed and again the law is quite specific. The maximum speed that a car may tow at is set at 50 mph for single carriageways and 60 mph on dual carriageways and motorways. Everywhere else you must obey the speed limits.

Before setting off it is important to ensure that the car and trailer are fully checked out and that all the lights and indicators work on the trailer board. If you have never towed before then find someone who has to either give you some instruction or go with you on your first trip. Also, make sure that the load on your trailer is secure and that there are no odd bits sticking out that overhang, in any direction, that may be a hazard to other road users. In other words be sensible about you loaded trailer, and if you require two trips to get everything shifted, then plan accordingly.

In general make sure that you drive smoothly and deliberately. When changing lanes give plenty of warning of your intentions and when moving back after overtaking another vehicle give more than ample room to allow a good space between you.

Pay attention to fuel levels, as you will see quite a drop in the economy of your car when towing.

The weather, and particularly the crosswind, can effect you quite severely so be prepared for this. Many caravans come to grief because of windy conditions and the weather must be well respected by all towing motorists.

Remember not to drive in the overtaking or fast lane of a motorway, because you are breaking the law and will be fined if caught.

When stopping, make sure that you do not obstruct entrances or in any way inconvenience other road users.

Watch your speed. Time and again motorists do not refer to their speedo often enough and they can find the road speed creeping up. Generally trailer axles and tyres are not designed for sustained high speed and problems can occur. A well-laden trailer with tyres slightly down on pressure driven too fast will cause tyre failure. It is back to being aware of what you are doing.

Study the regulations and ensure that you, your car and trailer are fit for the journey.

"Towing? Make sure she's not too big for you."

NOTE 27

TRANSPORTING ANIMALS

Before transporting any animal, ensure that you plan your journey. Some animals love travelling, especially dogs, many of them cannot wait to get into the family car. To them it is like 'walkies' without the effort. Many other pets do not fare so well. Cats seem anxious about it and a trip to the vet can be difficult. Make sure that 'Tiddles' is comfy in his or her travelling cage. A frightened or distressed animal loose in the car is both a distraction and dangerous if it gets caught up with the driver in some way.

Take the vets advice if you have to transport the family pet some distance. It is good sense to take a passenger when carrying a pet, unless the animal is well use to travelling with you.

Transporting large animals such as horses must be done with great care. Keep journey times short and check the animal at very regular intervals.

In the event of an accident, distress for the animal is considerable.

NOTE 28

TRANSPORTING CHILDREN

A very important item that is giving great concern is the fitting of child seats in cars. There are so many child seats available and so many different makes and models of cars that the whole system of fitting seats safely is becoming uncertain.

In the year 2000 over 16,000 children were injured in car accidents and it is estimated that 80 per cent of the child seats were incorrectly fitted.

We require a universal standard of fitting and the USA are already ahead with legislation that will make a safe fitting arrangement to all cars mandatory. I trust that we will follow suit. In the meantime, however, it is the best advice to carefully read the fitting instructions before fitting and then get advice from the car manufacturer as well as the seat manufacturer to ensure that you child is safe in the car. If you have any doubt then contact the AA or RAC who have experts who can give you the professional advice required.

Children of all ages can be a great distraction to the driver, and without doubt this has caused many accidents when the only adult in the car is driving.

A common mistake is to turn and look at little Johnnie on the back seat, whilst this happens the driver pulls at the steering wheel normally right hand down. This causes the car to swing to the right and on a single carriageway this can be fatal.

A simple test will demonstrate to you exactly what happens. Sit in the drivers seat whilst stationary and hold the steering wheel as you normally do. Your hands should be at about ten to two position. Now turn your head back to view the rear seats and note how much you move the steering wheel. If you find that hard to believe ask someone to watch you and comment on the amount you moved that wheel. You will be surprised.

Distraction is a major cause of drivers loosing control of their vehicles. Children can be the most distracting situation inside a car.

It is important to start teaching children the importance of what you, the driver, are doing. Tell them clearly that you must pay attention to what is happening on the road outside and they must behave to avoid distracting you. Children are not stupid and they soon will realise the importance of what you are telling them.

If you have to take a number of children out in a car then ensure that you have another adult with you to attend to them whilst you get on with the driving.

Remember to stop often on a long journey for comfort and drinks. Plan to keep them occupied with games or stories on tapes.

NOTE 29

PARKING AND BREAKDOWNS

So many drivers find it hard to park. To reverse into a gap between two parked cars is a task of nightmare proportions for some. The answer to this little problem is knowledge. Once a driver understands the reaction of the car to the drivers action input then the little problem is solved. Your instructor will have shown you and explained clearly to you what happens to the steering when you put the car into reverse. Remember what you have been taught and practise it.

Empty car parks that are lined out in bays are perfect for a little undisturbed practice. Select a bay to reverse into and position the car forward of the bay and reverse into it. It does not matter if you go over the lines or whatever the position you find yourself in. What matters is the fact that you are learning by practice how your car steers in reverse and the room required to manoeuvre safely into position. Do not hurry this exercise and slip the clutch to ensure a slow but controlled reverse movement into the bay. Sometimes it is much more convenient to drive straight into a parking bay. Do so if there are cars waiting behind you for spaces, for example in a multi storey car park. Often reversing out of this space is easier and a driver may feel more confident of this. Parking is all about confidence and when you get the hang of it you can be allowed to feel quite pleased with yourself.

Some criticism is levelled at drivers who park just a

little further out than necessary from the kerb. They should not be criticised so. It is a fact that many cars suffer damage to tyres, steering geometry and wheel edges through 'kerbing'. Steering damage should be avoided along with tyre wall damage. If anything goes wrong later you may rest assured that it will happen at speed and not in Sainsbury's car park. If you do accidentally hit or scrape the kerb then take your car to a tyre and wheel specialist and get it checked over. Out of alignment in the steering system can lead to heavy tyre wear as well as poor handling at various speeds.

If you have towed the Skylark down to the coast somewhere, ensure that you park your car and boat trailer in an appropriate spot so that you do not cause a major blockage to other road users. Just be considerate with boats and caravans.

If ever you breakdown then the first thing to do is get the car off the road if that is possible. If the engine stops but will turnover on the starter, engage first or reverse gear and wind the car forwards or backwards using the starter motor. There is more than enough power in the battery to accomplish this manoeuvre and get the car onto a verge. Cars stuck in the roadway are a hazard to other traffic, especially at night. If you do breakdown at night ensure that you leave your sidelights or parking lights on as well as you hazards. It is so important that other motorists are given as much time as possible to take the necessary action to safely avoid your car. Summon help with the mobile, and having done that, stay with the vehicle until assistance arrives. On motorways it is good advice to move away from the car and sit up on the embankment, in case your car is struck by other traffic. This regrettably often happens on motorways. If you have a red triangle then display it. Drivers approaching you vehicle need all the pre warning that they can get.

It is good advice to join one of the many recovery organisations that now exist and they back up the services that are offered by the AA and RAC. You know for sure that professional help is never far away.

NOTE 30

VEHICLE SAFETY AND SECURITY

Drivers must learn to be aware of the dynamic safety of their cars. Today's motor manufacturer has spent millions of pounds investing in designing, testing and manufacturing safety systems within the vehicle. Dynamic safety of the vehicle is now a predominant feature and for many years some motor manufacturers have sold their cars on the outstanding safety and protection that they offer the driver and passengers. The driver must take responsibility for completing the safety circle by ensuring that:

a) The vehicle is serviced and checked as required in the handbook by an authorised dealer.

b) Any damage to any part of the vehicle including tyres and wheels is inspected and checked out.

c) The correct oil and fuel is used.

d) All daily or weekly checks are carried out by the owner in line with the handbook recommendations.

I am surprised at the reluctance of some owners to carry out these checks. Normally the car is the second most expensive item that the average person buys after their house. The money that we collectively spend on buying cars, both new and second-hand is enormous and it seems unrealistic to neglect this valuable piece of machinery that we have parked outside the house. By checking the car you are doing two things, one, you are lessening the chance of a breakdown out on the road, and two, you are contributing to the dynamic safety standard of the car. By inspection you should notice damaged tyres, wheels, light lenses etc. The car manufacturer has done his job in supplying a safe vehicle for you and your family to travel in, so do your little bit to keep it as safe as it was designed to be.

Before every flight the pilot carries out a list of ground checks on the aircraft he or she is about to fly. Fondly known as 'kick the tyres and ping the wires' a complete documented list of items are checked and ticked off after proper inspection. If anything is noted as being unsatisfactory then the flight is cancelled and the fault is listed in the Technical Log for attention by a certified aviation engineer. The aircraft will not fly until the matter has been attended to and signed off. So please check your car.

Car security is getting more and more sophisticated as the number of stolen cars rises. The driver can help with this security by ensuring that the car is always locked when not attended, items of value are removed from the interior and placed in the boot or just taken away, and a visual deterrent fixed on the steering wheel or control pedals. Thieves happily inform anyone who cares to listen that they can get into a car in moments and disable any known device fitted in the car. That may be so, but they do shy away from cars with their registrations etched on the windows. A lot of theft is so called and 'joy riding' by young people. If a vehicle has enough preventive measures on show, then it is likely that another car may be selected for the 'joy ride'

There are many systems under development that will make it very difficult if not impossible to steal a car, and these are now coming onto the market in new cars. Already there is a trace signal system, so that a car may be tracked electronically, and for everyone's peace of mind this is a car security system to be recommended.

Be vigilant and be aware of car thieves. If your car is stolen it is likely to be either recovered damaged or burnt out. Possibly you may never see it again, but what you can be sure of is that the insurance settlement will be a lot less than you expect, so it will cause you some loss if your car is stolen. Do not let it happen through carelessness.

Over 370,000 vehicles were reported stolen in Britain in 1999. Older cars are more likely to be stolen as modern cars are now fitted with increasingly sophisticated anti theft devices. The figures of stolen cars reported are going down as new technology is slowly beating the car thief.

"...checks are carried out in line with the handbook."

NOTE 31

CAR CLEANING

The three things you see when you look at a car are the exterior shape, the colour and the trim inside. You can not do anything to alter these things, but by keeping the car clean inside and out you present a much more desirable car to own and to drive. Take any car you care to and think of it covered in road film, mud and general dirt with a filthy, untidy interior and you have something that you would not wish to drive or be seen in. Take a Bentley or an Aston Martin in this state and although they look dreadful they are underneath all that dirt fabulous cars and a delight to drive and own.

In simple terms a clean and well-presented car seems to go better and the driver feels good driving it. Keeping your car clean is important. There are some powerful safety reasons for keeping it so. First, a clean car has a windscreen, rear screen and side windows you can see out of clearly. Secondly, a clean car will have clear headlights, rear lights and indicators. Thirdly, the driver will feel good and comfortable driving this car. These are all valid reasons for a touch of cleanliness.

Cleaning the exterior paintwork.

For the best results follow these steps regularly:

a) Wet the car thoroughly with a low-pressure hose.

b) Using a large soft sponge wash the car down with a good quality car shampoo.

c) When you have thoroughly washed the car, starting on the roof panel and working down and around the car, rinse off with a low-pressure cold water hose.

d) Allow the water to drain down.

e) Using a good quality chamois leather, wipe the panels down, starting on the roof and follow the same pattern as the wash down with shampoo.

f) When thoroughly dry, inspect the paintwork for tar spots, flies and paint chips.

g) Clean off tar spots with a recommended tar remover or a little white spirit on a soft cloth.

h) Clean off flies with a light polishing compound.

i) Touch up any stone chips to prevent moisture getting in under the paint film and causing blistering.

j) Inspect the car paintwork carefully and when thoroughly clean and free of blemishes apply a good quality wax polish using soft mutton cloth.

k) Do not wax polish the car too often as a build up of wax may cause problems at a later date.

l) Note that all paint systems 'breathe' and they must be free to do so. Ensure you do not 'lock' any dirt or road film under the wax polished surface.

For the interior, keep it well vacuumed out and tidy. There are various trim and leather cleaners and restorers available on the market. You will be surprised at how much better you feel driving a clean car.

NOTE 32

CAR SERVICING

This is a very important and safety critical item. Proper servicing by an authorised agent is the only sure way to maintain the safety and reliability of your car. Many modern cars have electronic systems on board that can be checked and faults diagnosed by the agents and dealers who have the correct equipment and personnel on site to carry out the work.

Old Jim down the road may have been servicing cars for a hundred years but if he does not posses the equipment and expertise to service your car, then he can only do half the job. Things have moved on since the good old days!

It is certainly true that many small independent garages will take good care of your car and check it thoroughly for safety, but if they do not have all the equipment to set the car up and diagnose the engine state, then you may, for example, experience greater fuel use. The facts are that you have to go to a dealership or authorised agent for the service and to get your service book stamped. A fully stamped book enables you to sell the car with a full service history. This is important.

Many garages both large and small give less than satisfactory service to their customers. The last Office of Fair Trading (O.F.T.) report in 2000 stated that 1.3 million motorists complain annually about garages. The report states that 40 per cent give poor service and motorists spend £170 million on rectification work.

It is a concern that there are so many complaints and the industry needs to examine itself carefully and put some form of regulation in place to avoid a serious intervention by the government.

It is a good tip when you first start dealing with a garage or dealer of your choice that you inform them that you intend to be a regular customer if their work and service to you is satisfactory. They know then that you will remain loyal if they honour their responsibilities. As time goes by, the relationship can grow and be both pleasant and anxiety free. From my own experience, I can safely say that by purchasing my vehicles from my local dealer, RGR Garages Ltd, and ensuring that they service and repair my car to the exclusion of all else, I have enjoyed very good service and attention. This very satisfactory arrangement has been in place for fourteen years now, and I have had to complain only once that an item required further attention and it was done in an instant at no extra cost.

Do not be afraid to complain politely. If the car does not drive properly or you have any concern then return immediately to get it checked out. Generally, malfunctions do not improve if you ignore them. In aviation the saying is ' it doesn't get better after you've taken off'. The same applies to a car.

The servicing of all mechanical devices is highlighted once again in aviation. All aircraft must be checked and serviced at proper times as set down in the operators manual and must be signed off by a competent aviation engineer with the correct qualifications and ratings. It is the only way that reliability and safety can be assured.

NOTE 33

DRIVING PERFORMANCE CARS

I believe that it is not possible to drive high performance cars safely without professional tuition. Most drivers, especially young and inexperienced ones, believe that a performance car is the same as the average family saloon, but just faster. If drivers get behind the wheel of a performance car they soon find out that it is a very different beast indeed. Sometimes the results are fatal. There have been numerous occasions when misguided parents have bought something very special for their child, only for the matter to end in an accident. It is easily done.

Many high performance car manufacturers advise new owners to take an advanced driving course with their car or they provide tuition on a racing circuit themselves. This is the right approach for considerate ownership. Any car in the wrong hands is a lethal weapon and a high performance car multiplies the problem. To be out on the highway amongst other road users with such a vehicle is a great responsibility. Since I finished road testing of Aston Martin cars ten years ago, I have witnessed an increase in traffic volumes that would now make test driving during the day much more difficult.

It also must be remembered that with government legislation bringing in more severe penalties for motoring offences including speeding, the use of a performance car within speed limits in this country seems to be less interesting. Certainly continental use of high performance vehicles is much more attractive but I believe is limited in this country.

'...... legislation will bring in more severe penalties'

The exhilaration of incredible acceleration has to be experienced and sustained high speed becomes addictive, but all this activity must be in second place to road safety. The other alternative is to use the car on a racing circuit. There are clubs for all makes of car and it is good advice to join one, where help and information are available to an owner.

If you really want to enjoy the thrill of fast driving, then buy a Caterham Seven. These cars are the development of the Lotus Seven and are just about the closest you can get to a single seat racing car without the cost. These super whizzers are superb and very exciting to drive, and owners can join a very enthusiastic club who race and back up owners with help and advice at every level. Talk about acceleration and track handling! You will never have a dull moment, and on a properly organised circuit you will be safe and secure, that is, within the understanding that motor racing is dangerous. It is better to be there on the circuit than testing your skills on the busy roads of today.

To drive well you must be fit and very alert. The concentration levels required for performance handling are markedly higher and every driver who attempts this type of driving is soon quite tired and a little sweaty. Things to consider when road driving:

a) The acceleration rate will put you closer to hazards and other traffic so very quickly that you can be in a position of heavy braking consistently. This is both tiring and not particularly good for the car.

b) The driver must learn to scan the road ahead very quickly and take in the information that is being relayed back. The middle and far distance must be watched carefully, which makes the point that if anything occurs close to, such as a car pulling out of a side road without stopping, then immediate action must be taken to avoid a collision. Braking alone may not be enough at such close distance.

c) The use of engine power is closely coupled with the handling of the car and should be used in conjunction with the steering and braking.

d) Be aware that the whole driving experience is moving on to a much higher level, and this is where expert tuition is required to teach you the awareness and the need for quick reaction that is required to drive safely.

e) Be aware that other motorists who may be driving cars that are designated saloons and hatch backs, have extremely good performance, and will, without doubt, challenge you to drive fast and compete. It happens all the time and under no circumstances attempt to enter into this very dangerous activity. We had a strict rule at Aston Martin that if ever any other motorist challenged the Aston, I and the other two test drivers would pull over at the next convenient and safe place and commence filling in the in depth test sheets that accompanied the build of every car. The wonder racer would then slope off knowing that there would be no games on the road.

f) Weather and road conditions will play an even greater part in the safe control of a performance vehicle. Be aware.

The joy of ownership is a pleasant experience and if you drive the car as if you had just collected it from the showroom then with a little tuition you should enjoy safe and happy motoring.

As an example of how things go wrong so very quickly the following incident occurred in America. A new owner of an Aston Martin Lagonda parked the car in his garage and left his wife's car outside on the driveway. His wife asked if she could use the Lagonda and the owner readily agreed, but did not give her any instruction regarding the start up or the driving of the car. The lady wife duly climbed into the three and a half tonne machine and started the engine. She casually engaged reverse gear in the automatic box and released the handbrake. Thinking that she was driving just another big car with a lazy V8 engine, she accelerated. The massive power of the 5.3 litre engine whistled down the transmission and with the aid of the limited slip differential deposited all the power down on the garage floor. Reverse gear being the lowest ratio, it transformed the Lagonda into a space rocket and it propelled itself backwards at a speed that was almost immeasurable. The lady wife bounced off her car parked outside on the drive and luckily a little to the right of the emerging Lagonda, and proceeded down the driveway, across the suburban street, up the neighbours driveway opposite and crashed into his garage, demolishing most of it in the process.

A serious complaint was made and there was a full police and FBI investigation. The lady insisted that the throttle had jammed but after the closest mechanical examination it was shown to be free and working correctly. The findings were that the acceleration had been so rapid that the driver was subjected to negative G-force that made it impossible for her to lift her foot from the throttle. The point is, that no matter who was driving the Lagonda, the unexpected speed of the car took the driver by surprise. There is the lesson.

".....the unexpected speed of the car took the driver by surprise."

NOTE 34

SPECIALIST DRIVING SCHOOLS

It is a fact that the current and newly improved standard driving test is still not adequate and all embracing as it should be. Many good driving schools are encouraging pupils who have recently passed their test to carry on and have some further advanced instruction. This is excellent advice and is highly recommended. The test only touches the basics and it is just a licence to go solo. Back to aviation, after your first solo flight you then get down to the training that will enable you to fly to distant destinations, navigate correctly and carry passengers safely. Most of your flying training is after you have flown solo.

Every driver must gain experience, but at what cost? If a pupil has only just scraped through the test and maybe a little anxious about driving it makes great sense to encourage that driver to take on further tuition to improve skills and to gain confidence. An accident, no matter how minor, in these early days can shatter a driver's confidence and affect their ability. Once a driver has passed the test it is for life. Pilots are re checked every six months and tested through a whole range of emergencies and handling procedures. It would be a great step forward if the government had in place a refresher course at various intervals for all drivers. It could save lives.

There are now a number of advanced driving schools that

offer a variety of courses that may include circuit driving and skid control. These are excellent and are highly recommended. They make the ideal present for husbands and wives and you can be assured of expert tuition, learning a great deal and having a lot of fun. If a driver is really serious about their driving career and safe handling then one of these courses is a must. The opportunity to improve your skills are endless and I would encourage every motorist to attend a specialist school.

"...learn a lot, have fun and be a winner."

NOTE 35

OLD DRIVER'S REVIEW

My father purchased his driving licence before the Second World War for 25p at the Post Office. In those days you bought a dog licence and your radio licence all in the same little Post Office. You were not required to take a test and everyone was extremely relaxed about the whole situation. My father, after about five minutes tuition on how to start his car, a Morris Oxford Bullnose, was pointed in the right direction down the road and set off with my mother holding on grimly. So began his driving career. He always drove slowly and carefully and carried on in that fashion all his life. As the roads became busier he caused no end of congestion, and I can well remember as we drove down the A127 to Southend for a day out, that he shouted 'big shot!' at every motorist who whizzed passed at about 40 mph. My father was content to chug along at no more than thirty five mph. It took forever to get to Southend.

The lesson here is that things move on as progress is made and changes are part of the accelerating life we lead today. As motorists we must keep up and older and more mature drivers cannot rest on their laurels. It is every driver's obligation to all other road users to drive safely and to ensure that their actions do not adversely effect in any way the safety and flow of traffic. No one is too old to learn and that is a lifetime's occupation. An older motorist may have many years experience which will help in emergency situations or the early recognition that things are beginning to go wrong so that action to avoid an unpleasant accident can be put in place.

Without doubt motorists feel safer when driving because of the measures put in place by the motor manufacturers. We now have seat belts, disc brakes, air bags, side impact bars, high intensity lights, remarkable tyre compounds and stronger passenger compartments. The list goes on. However, this constant drive by the manufacturers to improve the safety of all occupants of the car must not allow the driver to engage in a mind set where there is an abdication of responsibility. You, the driver, are responsible to your passengers and other road users to drive properly and with care and attention. If you are an older person then you should ensure that you set a good example.

For more mature drivers there are a number of points to consider:

a) How medically fit are you?

b) Are you on medication that could effect your driving?

c) When did you last have your eyes checked?

d) Do you suffer with anything that may slow you down or restrict your movements?

e) How often do you drive?

f) How far do you drive in a year?

g) Have you considered the comparative costs of not owning a car but taking a taxi?

h) Do you own an old car?

i) Is it well serviced and checked?

j) Can you afford to maintain it properly?

It is sound advice to take someone who is a good driver and ask them to comment on your driving ability. Take advice and why not go to a driving school for an assessment.

Some men have two particular problems. One, they shy away from medical examination, unless they are pilots when they are stripped and gone over well and truly once a year. Two, they will not take tests or assessments, unless they are pilots when they are examined every six months. Why this is so I cannot imagine, unless it is foolish pride. I want to know if I am fit and so welcome my annual medical and I want to know that my flying skills are up to standard should the aircraft suffer a fire or malfunction. I also want to know if my driving is still safe and of good standard. Luckily I have a close relative who is a police Class One driver and he sits with me on regular occasions. He has informed me that as soon as he thinks I am sub standard he will tell me. Luckily he does not suffer from shyness.

I believe that at certain pre-determined ages, all drivers should have a medical and eye test. There also should be some form of driver assessment course which is compulsory. If all older drivers are as good as they think they are then no one will have a problem. It is estimated that 50 per cent of drivers require glasses for safe observation and driving. If they have got them they are not wearing them.

There are more elderly people in the population than ever before and as this trend continues then some government action must be taken to ensure that all elderly citizens who wish to drive must be fit and able to do so safely.

"...be a fit old driver – fit to drive."

NOTE 36

DRIVING IN EUROPE

We cannot wait to slip across that channel and get cracking in France and the rest of Europe. We all immediately think of cheap wine, excellent cheeses and sunshine. For some motorists, however, the first trip across to Europe can be daunting and a little unnerving. First, they drive on the wrong side of the road and secondly, don't speak the same language. Help!

Provided the driver plans the journey and takes advice, motoring in France and the rest of Europe can be a great pleasure. I do draw the line a little around the Coliseum in Rome where I have rushed round in ever decreasing and expanding circles as I have negotiated my way in and then out of the circular Italian traffic stream. Rome is a wonderful and quite fantastic city, but I do advise a driver to acquire some considerable experience before testing themselves in Rome.

Contact the AA or RAC to obtain information and advice. Simply follow the instructions and prepare yourself and your car for the impending adventure.

It has been my experience of driving in Europe that one should be cautious at first until the traffic speed and flow becomes second nature to you. It does not take long to settle in and once out of the Channel ports you will be delighted with the space and easy driving.

Garages and filling stations are helpful and it is a constant surprise how many Europeans speak English. They do have some respect if you try and speak to them in their own language and normally manage to shame you by replying in English.

When travelling on single carriageway roads you must keep well back to ensure that you have a good view of the road, and when attempting to overtake, be guided by your front seat passenger who should be able to tell you when you can move out a little to ascertain if it is safe to overtake.

Keep to the speed limits in and around towns. The police are vigilant and you will be fined on the spot without a moments hesitation. On the motorways it appears to be a little more relaxed, but be aware that speed limits exist in every country except in Germany at the time of writing.

There is plenty of space in Europe and your driving there should be very pleasurable.

NOTE 37

DRIVING IN THE USA

Driving in the USA is a wonderful experience except for the 55 mph speed limit. I must confess that whilst working over there for Aston Martin I found the speed limit very irritating with such wide open spaces. When one has the room for some fast driving and the car to do it with, it is a struggle to obey the law. But one must. I was stopped by the police on a number of occasions and I believe that was very much out of curiosity although they always said that it was a routine check. When they discovered that I was English and worked for the company they always became very friendly and asked to look around the car, especially at the motor under the hood. To see a hand built V8 engine was very interesting and quite quaint to them.

Most Europeans who drive in the USA are on holiday and are enjoying one of the popular fly and drive holidays that are becoming so popular. It is a great way to see the States in an unhurried and leisurely fashion. Once out of the major cities it becomes very pleasant motoring indeed.

Generally, once away from the major cities, your personal security is much less of a problem. Staying with friends up on Cape Cod it was interesting to see how relaxed they were about security.

There is a lot of good advice from the car rental

organisations, and the Americans really do enjoy tourists coming to the USA and having a good time. My experience is that they really work at it. Garages and roadside assistance are readily available and it appears that everyone is there to help.

Fuel is extremely cheap compared with Europe and Britain in particular making car travel a very inexpensive way of covering high mileages. The USA is the country of the automobile and luckily for them they have got the room to enjoy it.

NOTE 38

AIRBAGS

These safety devices are excellent and without doubt they are making a real contribution to reduce injuries to drivers and passengers. They are an explosive device that deploys a large inflatable bag in milliseconds to protect the occupants as they crash forward towards the steering wheel and dashboard.

Some problems have been identified that good drivers must be aware of.

If you are carrying a child in a child seat mounted on the front passenger seat with the child facing backwards, there is a real risk of injury to the child if the air bag deploys. Check this very carefully with your car manufacturer for sound advice on the fitting and positioning of the child seat.

If you are a little on the short side in stature, ensure that you do not sit too closely to the steering wheel. If the bag deploys and you are too close, then facial injury could result from the deployment. Designers of the system expect the driver to be sitting back from the full extent of the bag deployment and that the driver's head will move forward into the fully expanded airbag. In other words you must hit the airbag, it must not hit you.

The bag deflates quickly, having supported your head and upper torso during the impact.

Manufacturers are now fitting air bags to the side of the car in the door cappings. This is an extremely good development, as the survival from side impact collisions is as low as 15 per cent. Anything that improves driver or passenger safety from this dreadful situation is very welcome indeed.

Just be aware of the safe use of the airbag.

NOTE 39

TRAINING CHILDREN

Children will become the future drivers and road users of the world. It is a good idea to start training them in driving and road safety matters as early as possible. If by careful training we can reduce the accident rate, then let everyone who is a parent start now.

Children learn so quickly and it is desirable to acquaint them with the basics of road safety, coupled with good sense.

Education is a wonderful thing. Many years ago a drunk driver was regarded in a very different light than today. Anyone who drinks and drives is now looked down upon. In time that may be the case for speeding motorists. In other words the public and their opinion is being influenced by the good sense of not drinking and driving and now, speeding.

Children can be made aware of foolish actions of adults and they see very clearly the right and wrong way of doing things.

Motor vehicles are here to stay and whether in the future they are powered by fossil fuels or electricity or sunlight or atomic power, they are with us.

Let us start training the future drivers now.

Inform your children and get them interested in what you are doing as a good driver, for example:

a) Get them to help you check the car over for oil and fluid levels.

b) Get them to help you to wash the car and explain the relevance of being able to see the road through the screens.

c) Get them to help you plan the route on your journey to Aunt Nellie.

d) Make them aware of distractions.

e) Tell them what you are doing when you drive the car.

f) Give a running commentary on what you see as you drive along. This is extremely good practice for you as well as the children. You have to make a running commentary when you take your advanced driving test and the police examiners require it from the officers undergoing examination.

g) If they are keen to drive, and most young people are, then make sure you get them booked into a good driving school as soon as they have their provisional licence and are ready to drive.

h) Take an interest in your children's driving education. It may save their life one day.

It is important that children learn road safety by

instruction and understanding, and not by brutal and bitter experience. Ask traffic police or paramedics about how they feel when they attend a road traffic accident where children are trapped or injured. As parents themselves they find the situation harder to bear than imaginable. As a good driver, set the right example from the earliest age and ensure that your driving does not harm your children.

"......let them help wash the car and plan the route".

NOTE 40

THE POLICE

The police are not the enemy. They never have been. What they are is a service, which upholds the law by the consent of the population. They do not make the laws; Parliament does that on our behalf. When you vote for your selected parliamentary candidate just remember that he or she and their colleagues, if they come to power, are the people who decide what the speed limits should be, what by pass roads are to be built and most important, where all the road and fuel taxes go.

If you speed through a thirty mile an hour zone at fifty with the local school just turning out and you get caught on a radar trap, then tough, you are not a good motorist, you are an inconsiderate and dangerous one. The police have every right under the law to prosecute. I have heard numerous hard luck stories outlining the wicked Police in their attempts to hammer the unsuspecting motorist. Well, I have a comment to make. Having driven over 2 million miles in this country and abroad, I have not suffered any action from the police that I did not deserve. I have been caught for exceeding the speed limit on several occasions in my early days. I paid the fines and apologised to the magistrates. Each one 'was a fair cop guv.'

It is important for good drivers to keep in mind that traffic police are normally first on the scene of an accident and have to deal with all manner of unpleasant things from dead drivers to badly injured passengers. What would make any person hot under the collar would be the certain knowledge that some buffoon driving a car far too fast, carelessly or possibly whilst drunk, had caused the death and injury of perfectly innocent road user.

The government will continue to bring in harsher penalties for those who persistently break the law, our law remember, and injure other people and damage their cars. I must stress that it is only a mindless minority, but if they do not obey the law, then they must suffer the punishment.

If the traffic police stop you, then be aware that the first few moments of the conversation can affect the outcome.

The policeman is doing his duty, so be polite and as he represents the authority of the law be mindful of that. Start off on the right foot and listen without protestations or argument to what the officer has to say. You can be sure that if you have been stopped there is a good reason for it. Being courteous might just make the difference between a warning instead of some thing more serious. By all means put your point of view and you will be listened to, but in the final analysis you can be sure that you have been observed breaking the law.

Police are on patrol in unmarked cars and are looking for dangerous or inconsiderate motorists. The former face prosecution and the latter may get a warning. If a driver is seen to break the law or behave badly, then they can expect an order to stop from an ordinary saloon that suddenly displays blue flashing lights and a notice reading Police Stop. You have been warned. Motorists who drive too close or 'tailgate' others, particularly on motorways will get pulled when observed. Overtaking on the inside and swerving from lane to lane will bring the full weight of the law down on the stupid driver's head. Excessive speeding is a certainty for prosecution. The bad driver may have been filmed or on video and it is therefore foolish in the extreme to deny what may have just taken place. Everyone thinks that they can drive fast and that they are fantastic drivers, then pose the question, why do we have so many accidents in this country? If we had only a handful of accidents each year our insurance premiums would drop dramatically. The fact is that the vehicle repair industry turnover is measured in millions and millions of pounds. We still have far too many accidents, which is the proof that we are not that good.

It is your experience in life that shapes your thoughts and ideas. Many years ago I had a customer who ran a small vehicle paint shop with his wife and only son. They were very kind, mild and inoffensive people. One Saturday afternoon the son drove his Morris Minor 1000 over to collect his fiancé and return for dinner that evening. On the return journey a Ford Zodiac with three men in it, all of whom had been drinking heavily, came round a bend on the wrong side of the road and crashed head on to the Minor 1000. The young man and his fiancé were killed instantly. The police arrested the unbelievably unhurt drunks and the driver was handed down a jail sentence. The actions of these men destroyed these good peoples lives and I was deeply moved to see how fast they deteriorated after this tragic loss. They sold up and left the area some months later.

I was delighted that the police took the action they did in this case. We should always support the police in doing their duty because that is what we have asked them to do.

If the police instruct you to stop your car then do it as quickly and safely as you can. Complying with the police request promptly will ensure a good start to the conversation that is about to take place.

Police drivers are very highly trained and always remember that they observe good drivers as well as bad drivers.

Police throughout the world are trying different approaches to try and lessen the road casualties that bedevil modern life. In California, offending motorists are offered an opportunity to attend classes in how to be a better and safer driver instead of paying fines or going to prison. Most are opting for the course which is designed around a humorous approach to getting the message across. It is proving very successful, and without doubt the philosophy will be studied and the humour modified to meet the perceived needs of other states and countries.

Humour is a great conveyor of information, because people will remember funny situations and comments. It is back to being aware and remembering those vital, and possibly, life saving facts. Everyone has some resistance to boring facts but funny comments reduce everyone's barriers and so allow the free flow of information.

POINTS FOR CONSIDERATION:

- The police are not the enemy; do not treat them as such.
- Obey an order to stop quickly and safely.
- Listen to the officer politely.
- Make your point calmly.
- You have the legal right to go to court and challenge the prosecution if there is one.
- If you are a good driver then you are only ever likely to meet a traffic policeman off duty.

Good drivers will have no difficulty with the police as long as good drivers obey our laws.

CONCLUSIONS

As soon as I started driving in September 1957 I knew that all I wanted to do was to drive safely and enjoy motoring. The freedom that it offered was remarkable to me, and as the roads were comparatively free of traffic I looked forward to a long and happy driving experience. I could not have known that that would have been my fortunate future.

From the very outset I wanted to be fast and good at road driving and I worked hard to build up my experience and develop my skills. As I drove around the country and then onto the Continent, I realised how basic the driving test had been in preparing me for the situations that I encountered. I am even more critical of the test today, and I urge all new drivers who have just passed the test to take further instruction from their driving school to gain the knowledge and experience so necessary to be a good, safe driver. I think few drivers will follow that advice.

It is a fact that once a driver has passed the test, they are at liberty and within the law to immediately purchase a performance car, such as an Aston Martin or a Porsche, and drive straight onto a motorway The new driver has no experience or training to drive a high powered car on a motorway, but the law allows such a person to do this and carry passengers. This is the same as a pilot going solo in a Cessna and then being allowed to fly a Boeing 747 with passengers to some overseas destination. It quite frankly is both dangerous and illogical.

The only options to solving this problem are to either make the driving test much more comprehensive, with sign-offs by an instructor for a number of hours mandatory night driving and a number of hours mandatory motorway driving, under instruction. Alternatively, make it illegal for a new driver to use motorways until they had driven safely for a period of time and then obtained instruction on motorway driving. Also, make it illegal to drive any vehicle over a set engine size, for example 1600 cc, for a period of time and then any vehicle over 3000 cc for a further period of time.

Driving high performance cars on our roads safely is a very different situation than driving a modern small economical saloon that the learner driver would have used when under instruction and final test. It is extremely difficult and it demands great concentration to handle a high performance car. Without doubt any driver needs instruction to manage the complete change of parameters that surround such vehicles. Whilst being extremely exciting to drive, they are extremely dangerous in the hands of untrained and inexperienced drivers. The government should review this particular loophole as soon as possible.

I noticed as a young driver, that many motorists that I spoke to treated driving as 'not very important'. It was a means to an end, and as long as the car got you to your planned destination then it really did not matter too much how this was achieved. I formed the opinion that many people treated the car like a washing machine. You got in it, pressed a few buttons, pushed levers and set off.

They seemed to be oblivious of what was going on outside the car. They felt comfortable and safe within their domain, surrounded by creature comforts, and seemingly uncaring about the situation on the road before them. A rather aggressive driver who owned a large Volvo saloon informed me that he felt safe and comfortable in his car and believed that should he be involved in an accident, he would undoubtedly survive. It is true that Volvo have built very safe and robust cars, with strong passenger cells, air bags and side impact protection to ensure that driver and passengers have the maximum dynamic safety that Volvo are able to design and engineer into the car. This is of course is to be applauded. Volvo, however, are not responsible for the mindset of such drivers who may own their cars.

I asked this driver about other road users who may not be Volvo owners and would therefore suffer considerably in the event of an accident. Not my problem, he assured me. Well it is his problem, because this uncaring mindset means that his driving may be less than satisfactory. His attitude should be one of recognition of the fact that his large and powerful car must be driven with great care to ensure that other road users are not hurt by collision with his Volvo.

Safety and awareness of other road users needs go hand in hand, and only by driving to agreed standards of road behaviour will the accident rate fall. The basic bad driving faults are timeless and go on and on repeating themselves with the inevitable consequences of more road deaths and injuries. Just think for a moment of the number of people who may be affected by one person's death in a road accident. First, there is the immediate family and friends. Then relations, close and distant. Colleagues at work, perhaps customers and other work related acquaintances. Social contacts and others who know of the person. The list appears almost endless. For every one of the 100 people a week who are killed, many thousands more lie behind that dreadful statistic.

During the last forty-three years driving daily on our roads, I have come to the conclusion that the vast majority of motorists drive with care and consideration. A minority, however, either through aggression or ineptitude spoil the overall safe driving experience. It must be hoped that the government will continue to raise the penalties for these persistent and foolish drivers as well as recognising that the majority behave responsibly.

It is not difficult to be a good driver